To

*my husband, Paul,
whose love, support, and encouragement
make it possible for me to pursue
my call to write;*

*my mentor, Anne Sirna,
who has taught me more about the craft of writing
than anyone else;*

*my friend, Sue Cameron,
who has helped me stretch and grow;*

*and my writing papa, Lee Roddy,
whose challenge to
"Write so heaven will be different"
launched my writing ministry.*

"Write my answer on a billboard,
large and clear,
so that anyone can read it at a glance
and rush to tell the others."

Habakkuk 2:2, TLB

Contents

Foreword

This book can change your life. It not only gives on-going encouragement to respond to God's call to write, but helps you keep on writing. This book can also be used to deepen your walk with Him.

So I am pleased to introduce you to the book's author, Marlene Bagnull.

I met Marlene at a 1980 writers' conference where I was speaking and teaching. Marlene, like many, felt God's call on her life to write for Him.

At that time, I wrote a notation in Marlene's Bible about one of my own motivational verses: Habakkuk 2:2 and 3. There God says to "write the vision."

In the margin of Marlene's Bible alongside that verse, I wrote, "This was God's promise to me as an author. Maybe yours, too?"

Marlene was sure God had called her to write a book, so she set down her vision. That's not uncommon. Many writers, filled with inspiration, start off strong. Then they get discouraged and quit. When they do, God's vision for them is lost. How sad!

If it's God's will to write, then it's logical that publication should eventually follow. After all, an unfinished manuscript cannot change lives. Even a finished script cannot minister in a drawer or filing cabinet.

Only in published form can a book go where you and I will never go, to people we will never meet. Only in published form can a book make a difference in eternity.

So why do many writers, feeling called to write, fall short? I believe it's because they neglect to note the way God says He will bring the vision to pass. That involves His time element, not the writer's. Read the Lord's clear words:

"But these things I [God] plan won't happen right away. Slowly, steadily, surely, the time approaches when the vision will be fulfilled. If it seems slow, do not despair, for these things will surely come to pass. Just be patient! They will not be overdue a single day!" (TLB).

I don't know of a single successful author in the inspirational field who hasn't experienced doubts and discouragement. The unsuccessful are the ones who quit.

Marlene did not quit. She was faithful. She kept her commitment and obeyed her "call," even though she suffered through some very, very discouraging times. Hard times. Testing times. Learning times.

God gave Marlene the reward of a published book, then another, plus the seed for this one. But this isn't a book about Marlene; it's a book about you, the "called" writer.

This devotional book for writers (published or unpublished) is designed to inspire and give encouragement for those difficult times which all writers face. It's a work planned to help you fulfill your "call" and see the fruits of your labors.

Please join Marlene as she leads you through her unique devotionals for writers, for this book can change your life.

Lee Roddy
Penn Valley, CA

*"Write my answer on a billboard,
large and clear, so that anyone can read it
at a glance and rush to tell the others."*
Habakkuk 2:2, TLB

1
Called to Write

Our neighborhood was no longer quiet or safe. A group of rowdy teens had claimed it. After a night of their partying, empty beer cans littered our manicured lawns. It also was not at all uncommon to find paint sprayed on cars, flat tires, and smashed lawn furniture. The targets for their vandalism were those who dared to suggest that they quiet down or go someplace else.

"What next?" we wondered and worried, especially when it became evident that drugs were involved. We knew we should do something, but what? The police regularly patrolled, but they seemed as helpless as we felt.

One night the kid brother of a gang member climbed a pole by the trolley stop and was electrocuted by the wires above the tracks. He was only thirteen years old! "Oh God," I wept, "was there something I could have done that might have saved his life?"

I've asked similar questions when I've viewed documentaries on world hunger, homelessness, alcohol and drug addiction, AIDS, child abuse, and the aging. But the problems are so big and I again feel so helpless.

The family--the most basic and important unit of society--is under attack. Christian homes are far from immune. Divorce, adultery, the battering of women and children, incest, and teen suicide happens in our homes, too. Immorality is rampant. Violent crime is increasing. Our environment is being destroyed. And our children, both before and after birth, are at risk.

Where is God? What is he doing about it? I believe he's calling people like you and like me to: "Write my answer on a billboard, large and clear, so that anyone can read it at a glance and rush to tell the others" (Hab. 2:2, TLB).

When the Lord first brought this verse to my attention, I was not at all certain he was speaking to me. I knew Jesus Christ as my Lord and Savior. I knew without a doubt that he is the answer to man's deepest needs, but I doubted my ability to write that answer in a compelling and effective way. I had never gone to college or taken a course in creative writing. I also had never shaken the enormous inferiority complex I'd been carrying since childhood. It didn't take me long to conclude that he must have meant that verse for someone else.

Then I recalled a familiar Scripture: "If anyone publicly acknowledges me as his friend, I will openly acknowledge him as my friend before my Father in heaven. But if anyone publicly denies me, I will openly deny him before my Father in heaven'" (Matt. 10:32-33, TLB).

Certainly my refusal to write was not a denial of him, or was it? "Lord," I prayed, "you know I don't ever want to deny you, but I don't see how I..."

"It's not a question of your ability," I felt him assure me. "You really can do everything I ask you to do with the help of Christ who will give you the strength and power" (see Phil. 4:13, TLB).

I tried a whole bunch of "but Lord" excuses. They all sounded hollow next to his promise to help me. "But," I continued to argue, "I don't even know *what* you want me to write. I know you're the answer, but how do I say that in a way that someone will publish?"

"Write out of your life experiences," I felt the Lord say to me. "Make yourself transparent and vulnerable so others can see what I have done, and am doing, in your life."

The choice was clear. The Lord had given me my instructions. To refuse would be an act of disobedience. Yet, it wasn't easy to admit on paper, for the world to read, that I often failed to handle both big and little problems in a Christ-like way. I didn't want people to know that I'm not a model Christian, that my faith falters, and that some days I feel overwhelmed and inadequate. But I also knew the Lord had taught me many things through my struggles--lessons that could perhaps be used to help someone else.

I swallowed my pride and began to write about "Battling and Defeating Depression," "Coping with Ingratitude," and "Praying About Everything." I discovered that the answers he'd given me could be a source of help and reassurance to others who also asked: "What's the Matter with Me?" or "Do I Have to Be That Honest?"

Making myself more vulnerable, I began to write about my life as a wife and mother. I admitted that "It Takes Two to Tangle" and that sometimes I'm guilty of "Taking It Out On the Ones I Love." I sensed that the most difficult things for me to share could be the very words someone else needed to read. Yet, the more prolific I became, the more my mailbox was stuffed with returned manuscripts. Sometimes they came back faster than I thought the U.S. Postal Service could deliver them! Others, like my first book manuscript, sat on an editor's desk for five months only to be returned with a form rejection slip.

"Do you think it was easy for me to go to the cross?" the Lord asked me one day when I grumbled about the mail. Stung by the truth of his words, I immediately apologized for forgetting how much he had suffered for my salvation.

"Neither is it easy for you to follow in my footsteps," he said gently. "But what I ask you to do, and what I will enable you to do, is to 'put aside your own pleasures and shoulder your cross, and follow me closely. If you insist on saving your life, you will lose it. Only those who throw away their lives for my sake and for the sake of the Good News will ever know what it means to really live'" (Mark 8:34-35, TLB).

Real living--from the world's standpoint, the life of a Christian writer hardly measures up. Few of us will achieve fame or fortune, or even earn a minimum wage for the hours we sit before our typewriters or word processors. But in the light of eternity, long hours, poor pay, and rejection slips mean nothing if even one life is touched.

The needs are urgent and, I believe, the time is short. We dare not assume that we will always have the freedom to print and distribute Christian literature. "'All of us,'" Jesus said, "'must quickly carry out the tasks assigned us by the one who sent me, for there is little time left before the night falls and all work comes to an end'" (John 9:4, TLB).

I still feel inadequate. I still doubt my abilities, but I do *not* doubt the One who has called me. I am choosing to risk and persist, knowing that "'Slowly, steadily, surely, the time approaches when the vision will be fulfilled. If it seems slow, do not despair, for these things will surely come to pass. Just be patient! They will not be overdue a single day!'" (Hab. 2:3, TLB).

Responding to God's Call to Write

Do you believe God has called you to write his answer? Why or why not?

What issue most deeply concerns you? Is there something God may want to say through you?

What is the biggest thing that causes you to doubt that he can use you?

Use the Bible Study Helps on pages 89-90 to further explore your calling. In the space below write out, and then commit to memory, the verse that speaks most strongly to you.

Keep your eyes on Jesus, our leader and instructor.
Hebrews 12:2, TLB

2
Look to Jesus

We are literature missionaries! While we may never go more than a few hundred miles from our home, our written words can go around the world and make a difference for all eternity.

The opportunities are great. The need to look to Jesus, "our leader and instructor" (Heb. 12:2, TLB), is even greater. It is his life and death and resurrection that inspires us to keep on keeping on and provides the pattern we need to follow, if we are to be effective communicators of his truth.

1. *Spend time in prayer.* While the Gospels only give us glimpses into the prayer life of Jesus, it is obvious his ministry was bathed in prayer. Prior to his first preaching tour, he got up long before daybreak in order to go alone into the wilderness and pray (see Mark 1:35). In the midst of a demanding ministry he "often withdrew to the wilderness for prayer" (Luke 5:16, TLB). He even spent an entire night in prayer before choosing the Twelve (see Luke 6:12).

Jesus' example shows us that the place to begin *all* our writing is on our knees. It is essential that we seek the "mind of Christ" (1 Cor. 2:16, TLB) if we hope to bring his answer to our hurting world. If we're too busy to pray, we're too busy. If we think we can shirk this necessary first step, we'll find that our words and paragraphs--no matter how well composed--will lack power. Prayer was an essential part of Jesus' preparation for ministry. So, too, it must be for us.

2. *Know what God's Word says and means.* The Bible is silent about Jesus' childhood except for the story of his trip to Jerusalem and how he amazed the teachers of the Law with his understanding of the Scriptures (see Luke 2:41-47). After his baptism, Jesus used the Scriptures to defeat Satan (see Luke 4:1-12). Throughout his ministry, Jesus often referred to the Law and the Prophets. Unlike the "religious" people of that day, Jesus not only quoted the words of Scripture, he brought clarification and fulfillment to them. He put the spirit back into the Law!

Unless we daily spend time in God's Word, our understanding of it will be shallow. Our attempts to write material to help and encourage others will be mere spiritual Band-Aids if, instead of the powerful promises of Scripture, our manuscripts are filled only with our opinions. It is the Word of God that convicts and changes people as well as prepares them to face the problems and challenges of daily living (see Heb. 4:12; 2 Tim. 3:16-17). Unless we ourselves are hungry for God's Word and partake of it daily, we cannot hope to inspire our readers to take it seriously.

3. *Have a vision.* Jesus knew why he had come and what he was called to do. Every word he spoke and everything he did was aimed at bringing glory to the Father (see John 17:4). He chose to become "obedient to death--even death on a cross!" (Phil. 2:8, NIV).

As writers we also need a vision. "Where there is no vision, the people perish" (Prov. 29:18, KJV)--and so do we as writers. We need to wait before the Lord for him to give us direction for our writing ministry. When we're discouraged and we doubt anyone will publish our work, he will enable us to remain obedient to the vision. He will remind us that faith is "the confident assurance that something we want is going to happen. It is the certainty that what we hope for is waiting for us, even though we cannot see it up ahead" (Heb. 11:1, TLB).

4. *Don't cut yourself off from people and their needs.* Jesus willingly "laid aside his mighty power and glory, taking the disguise of a slave and becoming like men" (Phil. 2:7, TLB). Once here, he did not cloister himself in the Holy of Holies. Instead, he walked and talked, laughed, ate, and wept with those around him. He knew their needs because he was one with them.

There is always a danger that the very nature of our work as writers will cause us to become hermits. It takes time to write, but sometimes we may take too much time. Our lives may get out of balance. We need to remember that our words will become glib and empty if we lose touch with real people and their needs.

5. *Know your audience and find ways to communicate effectively.*
Jesus used down-to-earth illustrations from everyday life. He was
observant of what was happening around him--a man sowing in his field,
a woman baking bread, a widow giving her mite. He used these experiences to bring home his points. Parables, or stories, became Jesus'
vehicle for teaching truth on many levels. Even the youngest child could
understand the story of the prodigal son or the good Samaritan, yet the
depth of these stories and their application to our lives continue to be discovered.

We, too, must know our audience. Are our potential readers young
or old? Male or female? Single or married? High school or college
graduates? Will the illustrations we use have meaning for them? Are
we training ourselves to be observant of what is happening around us and
using these observations to make our points effectively? Are we learning
to *show* instead of *tell*--in other words, to effectively use stories to present
our message?

Jesus used everyday language. One didn't have to be a scholar to
understand what he was saying. Are we addressing our readers at their
level of understanding, being careful not to write down to them but neither
to write above their heads? Is our language clear and readily understandable? Do we perhaps need an English refresher course to hone our writing
skills? Most important of all, are we trusting in the mighty power that is
present in the "simple message of the cross of Christ" (1 Cor. 1:17, TLB),
or have we been cluttering it up to impress our readers with our theological
understanding and knowledge?

6. *Learn to persist.* Some of our work, like that of the most gifted
authors, will be rejected. Yet again, we need to look to the Lord and his
example.

Jesus' very *life's* work was rejected by the people he came to save
(see John 1:10-11). Because it was no easier for Jesus than it is for us,
he is wonderfully able to understand and help us (see Heb. 2:18; 4:15).
Beyond that, he has given us his promise that in and through him we *will*
do even greater things (see John 14:12). As we ask him for help and seek
to follow his example, our writing and our lives will truly be an inspiration
to others.

Responding to God's Call to Write

What is the present condition of my prayer life?

How much time am I spending in the Word?

Have I sought the Lord for a vision for my writing? If so, am I walking in obedience to that vision?

Am I in touch with people and their needs?

Am I doing all I can to effectively communicate with my audience by writing and re-writing each piece until it is my very best work with no wasted words or weak phrases?

Am I willing to persist, or do I expect the Lord to somehow make it easy?

"But when the Holy Spirit has come upon you,
you will receive power to testify about me with great effect...."
Acts 1:8, TLB

3

By My Spirit

The events of the past week had left the disciples reeling. Their Master had entered Jerusalem thronged by a crowd shouting "Hosanna." Less than a week later another crowd shouted, "Crucify him." He left Jerusalem carrying a cross.

Then the impossible happened. Jesus rose from the dead! They saw him, touched him, broke bread with him. He was alive! And he had commissioned them to "'go and make disciples in all the nations'" (Matt. 28:19, TLB).

The power of the Resurrection and its call to commit ourselves to the living Christ has not diminished in 2,000 years. One Easter, after an intense struggle, I surrendered my life to him and took the plunge into the baptismal waters. Each year since, Easter has been a special time of renewing my commitment to share the Good News that Jesus is alive. He is "'the Way--yes, and the Truth and the Life'" just as he said (John 14:6, TLB).

But what happens to my commitment and enthusiasm--and yours, too, perhaps--during the time between our mountaintop experiences? As Christian writers, how do we rekindle our resolve to go into the world through our writing when it seems like everything we write is being rejected? Where do we find the determination and strength to persevere --to keep writing, keep submitting, and keep believing our words will one day get into print?

Jesus knew his disciples well. He knew they were just ordinary men who would need extraordinary power for the task before them. It wasn't going to be easy to reach a world. Although many would believe and be saved, countless others would be infuriated and threatened by the message of the Cross. In their own strength, the disciples could not hope to endure the persecution that awaited them.

The disciples undoubtedly had plenty of questions and doubts--the same as us. I suspect some must have felt panicky when Jesus ascended into heaven. Now what? How could they do what he called them to do without him beside them?

"'But when the Holy Spirit has come upon you, you will receive power to testify about me with great effect,'" Jesus had promised (Acts 1:8, TLB).

The message to us is clear. If the men who walked and talked with Jesus needed the Holy Spirit, how much more do we need him today!

We need him to sanctify us--to make us holy and acceptable vessels through which Jesus Christ can work (see Rom. 15:16; 1 Cor. 6:11). Often uncertain of the direction we should go, we need his guidance (see Gal. 5:16). In the face of disappointment and discouragement, some days maybe even despair, we need his comfort (see John 14:16). We need his power to persevere (see Rom. 15:13).

Challenged by conflicting theologies and the subtlety of humanistic ideas, we need him to reveal to us God's truth (see John 14:17; 15:26; 16:13). We need him to be our teacher if we are to teach others--to bring to our attention the lessons we have learned, and to show us how to effectively share them with our readers (see John 14:26). We need the "Holy Spirit's words to explain the Holy Spirit's facts" (1 Cor. 2:13, TLB). We need the thoughts and "mind of Christ" (1 Cor. 2:16, TLB) that we might write with sensitivity and understanding. And, tempted to preach, we need to be reminded that he alone convicts men of their sin and offers them the hope of God's redemption (see John 16:8).

Standing in need of all this and more, the question becomes, "Do we wait long enough to receive everything God wants to give us?" The disciples waited in prayer in the Upper Room for several days after Jesus' ascension. To be honest, I find it difficult to wait even for several minutes.

Far too often, my time at the word processor is prefaced by only a quick token prayer. I ask for the Lord's help and for his Spirit's anointing, but I fail to wait for him to fill me. I fail to heed the literal translation of Ephesians 5:18 to, "keep on being filled with the Holy Spirit." Even though it's evident that I "leak"--that I need repeated fillings of the Spirit's power--I don't sit still long enough for him to pour himself into me.

If we truly want God's power to infuse our writing and every aspect of our lives, we must learn to wait quietly in his presence. I have a hard time being quiet. I'm almost always on the go--always rushing. Even when I do sit still, my mind isn't still. Yet, I know I cannot sidestep the importance of first being filled if I hope to write anything that will have a lasting impact. I need his anointing so that every word, every sentence, is written with the "strength and energy that God supplies, so that God will be glorified through Jesus Christ" (1 Pet. 4:11, TLB).

The ways each one of us experience the power of the Holy Spirit in our life will be different, just as the gifts he gives us will be different. "There are many ways in which God works in our lives," Paul told the Corinthians, "but it is the same God who does the work in and through all of us who are his" (1 Cor. 12:6, TLB). We don't need to compare ourselves with anyone else or covet anyone else's gift because "Christ has given each of us special abilities--whatever he wants us to have out of his rich storehouse of gifts" (Eph. 4:7, TLB).

God longs for us to come into his presence, to open, and to use the gifts he gives us. By his Spirit we, too, can be his witnesses--in our Jerusalem, Judea, Samaria, and even to the ends of the earth (see Acts 1:8).

Responding to God's Call to Write

Study the following passages. Beside each reference note what the Holy Spirit is promising to do in your life. Then ask yourself if you are experiencing this aspect of being filled with and walking in the Spirit.

John 14:15-16

John 14:17, 26; 15:26; 16:13-14

Acts 1:8

Romans 15:13

Romans 15:16; 1 Corinthians 6:11

1 Corinthians 2:4, 10-16

Galatians 5:16

Galatians 5:22

Ephesians 4:7

Take time right now to wait in his presence and to ask him to empower
you anew for the work he is calling you to do.

*Roll your works upon the Lord--commit and trust them wholly to Him;
[He will cause your thoughts to become agreeable to His will, and]
so shall your plans be established and succeed.*
Proverbs 16:3, AMP

4

Making It Happen

I am the Bread of Life. I am the Light of the world. I am the Good Shepherd. Jesus did not have an identity crisis! He knew who he was and why he had come. Regardless of circumstances, or the opinions of others, he affirmed that he was the great "I Am" who existed before Abraham.

There are many "I am's" we can also affirm. We have no problem with some: I am a man or woman. I am a husband or wife. I am a father or mother. Neither do we have difficulty with "I am's" such as: I am a member of Fifth Street Church or the PTA.

As Christians, we can affirm still others: I am a believer. I am saved. I am forgiven. But as we move into the area of feelings and life goals, our "I am's" tend to become cloudy. "I am a witness for Christ" might be prefaced by the word, "sometimes." And even if we *know* God has called us to write, the statement, "I am a writer," might stick in our throats or be qualified by such words as "I think" or "I hope to be." Even established writers have days when they don't *feel* like writers--days when the fruit of their labors may not seem evident.

This spring my husband and I planted a vegetable garden. As I dropped seeds into holes and pushed dirt around tender seedlings, I could see vine-ripened tomatoes and glossy, deep purple eggplants. We also need to be able to see the writer we hope to become and the work we hope to produce for the Lord's glory. More importantly, we need to see the writer God wants us to become.

I'm not talking about using visualization techniques, but rather about a scriptural principle: "For as he thinks within himself, so he is" (Prov. 23:7, NASB). I have seen it proven many times. When I get up on the "wrong side of the bed" and picture myself becoming irritable with the children and getting nothing accomplished, my expectations are not disappointed. What I think in my heart is what I become! But what is true of negative thoughts, is also true of positive ones. When my mind is centered on Christ, and when I choose to rely on "his mighty power" I discover that he is able to do far more than my "highest prayers, desires, thoughts, or hopes" (Eph. 3:16,20, TLB).

Making it happen involves more than just desiring to see it happen. It also takes realistic and *planned* action. Periodically I take time apart with the Lord to assess where I'm at and where I need to be heading. I find it helpful to first set long-range goals. What is God's overall plan and purpose for my writing? Where does he want me to be five years from now? From there I break it down into specific and measurable short-term goals. When I first started writing, those goals included: Growing in my Christian walk, keeping a daily journal, studying the craft of writing, researching the markets, and completing that first manuscript. The first four goals have been, and must be, ongoing. The fifth one has been frequently changed and enlarged to reflect new writing challenges.

It has been said, "Attempt something so big that without God's help it will surely fail." In other words, it is important to stretch beyond our own capabilities; otherwise the challenge of our goal may not be enough to motivate us to accomplish it. For example, one year I set a goal of losing a pound a week. That seemed easy enough. Within a year I could be down to my desired weight. But I soon discovered I was gaining instead of losing! Why? I had made the goal so easy (or so I thought) that I didn't see the need to work at it. It wasn't until I revised my goal to two pounds a week that I stopped fooling around and began to make progress.

Next, we need to take a big step of faith and verbalize our goals to others. That's scary! I can still remember the first year I went to a

Christian writers' conference and told people about the book I planned to get published. Although it certainly must have been obvious that I had a lot to learn before I could hope to write a book, the instructors encouraged me to work at it. Other writers promised to pray for me.

Another step in reaching our goals is to determine the necessary spiritual and practical preparation. Do we need to become more disciplined in our study of God's Word? Are we actively involved in a strong body of believers? Practical preparation might include taking an English refresher course, attending a local creative writing class, enrolling in a correspondence study program (see page 96), joining (or even forming) a Christian writers' critique group.

Anticipating obstacles is another important step. I ask myself how I will overcome them. For instance, the telephone. I love to talk and I hate answering machines. I said I would never get one. Instead, I tried monitoring the length of my calls during "business hours." I tried and failed! Just like the computer I also said I never wanted, I've found that an answering machine is a real time saver.

I find it is essential to regularly review my goals. Tucked away in a bottom drawer they will be useless. "Check up on yourselves" the Bible says (2 Cor. 13:5, TLB). This passage goes on to ask other important questions. "Are you really Christians? Do you pass the test? Do you feel Christ's presence and power more and more within you? Or are you just pretending to be Christians when actually you aren't at all?" More important than whether or not we realize our goals and sell X number of manuscripts, is the manner in which we do our work and the foundation upon which we build our writing ministry. We can never become so consumed by our goals--by what we want to do for the Lord--that we neglect our relationship with him.

Prayerfully setting goals, putting them in writing, sharing them with others, and determining the specific things we need to do to make them happen is just the beginning. Then, as David told Solomon when he gave him the blueprints for building the temple, we need to: "Be strong and courageous and get to work. Don't be frightened by the size of the task, for the Lord my God is with you; he will not forsake you. He will see to it that everything is finished correctly'" (1 Chron. 28:20, TLB).

I am a writer! I am endeavoring to present the Good News through the words I write. I am matching my prayers with hard work. When I get discouraged, I am learning to trust in and rely on God. Whether I feel like it or not, I am choosing to embrace God's call to write and trusting him to make it happen.

Responding to God's Call to Write

Enlarge the goal planning chart that appears below. Go before the Lord and ask him to show you the goals he wants you to set.

Specific Goals	Spiritual Preparation	Practical Preparation	Expected Obstacles	How I Will Overcome
Weekly				
Monthly				
One Year				
Five Years				

Commit everything you do to the Lord.
Trust him to help you do it and he will. --Psalm 37:5, TLB

Put on the full armor of God so that you can take your stand
against the devil's schemes.
For our struggle is not against flesh and blood....
Ephesians 6:11-12, NIV

5
Put on the Armor

My hands tied behind my back, I was dragged before a tribunal of cloaked men. They accused me of subversion against the state because of my faith in Jesus Christ. I could not deny the charges, for spread across the table were books and articles I had written.

The congregation's singing brought me back to reality. Had I dozed off or seen a vision? I'll never know. But I do know the Lord spoke to me. "Do you realize, child," I felt him say, "that the things you are writing may one day convict you? Are you willing to follow me despite the cost?"

I didn't answer quickly or feel very brave when I finally gulped, "Yes, Lord."

That was seven years ago. Morally, things were bad and getting worse, but Christians generally were seen as part of the answer--not the problem. We were not the frequent brunt of jokes on TV sitcoms and talk shows. Media coverage was not as openly biased. The New Age was beginning to infiltrate some churches, but few discerned the danger of it or the occult.

Things are changing--rapidly. We can no longer ignore all the signs that point to the return of Christ. They challenge us to be actively involved spreading the Gospel while the doors remain open to produce and distribute Christian literature. But we do need to count the cost. In a very real way, writing for the Lord puts us on the front lines where "our struggle is not against flesh and blood, but against the rulers, against the authorities, against the powers of this dark world and against the spiritual forces of evil in the heavenly realms" (Eph. 6:12, NIV). To go into battle without the "full armor of God" (Eph. 6:11, NIV) is as foolish as a soldier entering the front lines dressed for a game of tennis. Having been defeated too often, I'm learning to pray on the armor every morning that I might "resist the enemy whenever he attacks, and when it is all over...still be standing up" (Eph. 6:13, TLB).

"Lord," I pray, "help me to gird myself with your 'belt of truth'" (Eph. 6:14, NIV). "Give me discernment that I might immediately recognize the enemy's lies and half-truths. Help me to refuse to receive or believe them." When a manuscript is returned and those insistent inner whispers threaten to defeat me, I buckle the belt of God's truth more tightly around me. I affirm, often out loud, that the return of one manuscript (or dozens of manuscripts) does not mean I should quit writing. I know God has called me to write and I'm working at developing the gifts he has given me. I also know that "God's gifts and his call can never be withdrawn; he will never go back on his promises" (Rom. 11:29, TLB).

The "breastplate of righteousness" (Eph. 6:14, NIV) protects my most vulnerable area--my heart, the home of my feelings and emotions. It is so easy for me to be wounded by others, to allow myself to be influenced by fear of what they might say or think. It is also easy for me to give in to the temptation to compromise, because "everyone else is doing it." I cannot pad my writing expenses on Schedule C. I cannot fail to attribute a quote just because it's only one or two lines. Instead, I must handle every aspect of the business side of my writing in a way that honors the Lord. My first priority must be to bring glory to him and not to myself. "Lord," I pray, "help me today to consistently choose to do what is right in your eyes. Thank you for protecting me from the judgment and criticism I may receive."

Putting on the shoes of readiness to share the Gospel (see Eph. 6:15) protects me from the temptation to get side-tracked. There are often other things I can do and write that would require less time and effort; but if I am to be a soldier of the King, I must take my orders from him. I need to follow his marching plan instead of asking him to bless mine. When I walk in obedience, I find that my feet do not become bruised and weary from going places he never intended me to go. I also find that when I say "yes" to what he wants me to do, rather than "yes" to what others tell me I should do or what I feel they expect me to do, I am filled with peace instead of tension.

I prayerfully pick up the "shield of faith" to "extinguish all the flaming arrows of the evil one" (Eph. 6:16, NIV). I ask God to make me mighty in spirit--to help me to walk by faith, not by sight. I also ask him to help me not to lower my shield by nurturing doubts. A soldier can be fatally wounded if he lowers his shield for only a moment.

The "helmet of salvation" (Eph. 6:17, NIV) protects my thought life. Each morning I thank God that I do not have to be bound by old habits and thinking patterns. I ask him to continue his work of transforming me by renewing my mind (see Rom. 12:2) and giving me the "thoughts and mind of Christ" (1 Cor. 2:16, TLB).

Finally, there is the one offensive piece of armor. It is with the "sword of the Spirit, which is the word of God" (Eph. 6:17, NIV) that we go forth into battle to confront the evil of our day. That doesn't mean we are supposed to hit our readers over the head with the Bible. Instead, I pray that God's Word will so permeate my life that the principles of Scripture will be evident in all I write, as well as in all I say and do.

"The enemy is within the gates," Chuck Colson writes in *Against the Night* (Servant Publications, 1989). "I believe that we do face a crisis in Western culture, and that it presents the greatest threat to civilization since the barbarians invaded Rome." But God commands us to trust him. Even when facing the "spirit of the antichrist," we need not fear because "the one who is in [us] is greater than the one who is in the world" (1 John 4:3-4, NIV). We need to "pray all the time" (Eph. 6:18, TLB) and to "be strong in the Lord and in his mighty power" (Eph. 6:10, NIV) knowing that Jesus has already won the battle.

Responding to God's Call to Write

Study Ephesians 6:10-18 in several translations or paraphrases. Ask the Lord to show you what each piece of the armor can mean in your life. List those insights below and begin to daily pray on the armor.

Belt of truth

Breastplate of righteousness

Shoes of readiness

Shield of faith

Helmet of salvation

Sword of the Spirit

Dreaming instead of doing is foolishness,
and there is ruin in a flood of empty words....
Ecclesiastes 5:7, TLB

6
Overcoming Procrastination

I groaned as I read the note at the bottom of the printed rejection slip: "I'm sorry, but we recently purchased a similar manuscript."

This wasn't the first time I missed out on a sale because I waited too long to develop an idea and get it in the mail. Like most writers, I tend to procrastinate, often without realizing it. I am a typical Type A personality, an achiever, a true workaholic. Yet, when I stop long enough to evaluate my accomplishments, I know that I have not always done, or written, that which is most important in the Lord's eyes.

The Merriam-Webster Dictionary definition of procrastination reads: "To put off usually habitually the doing of something that should be done." While some of us procrastinate more than others, few of us (if we are honest) can say we are immune. For a myriad of reasons, we tend to put off doing things--especially, it seems, getting words on paper. It's no wonder God seems to call a number of people to write similar things. He knows how few will actually finish what they start.

"O Lord, you have examined my heart and know everything about me," I read in Psalm 139:1 (TLB). I cannot hide from him my problem with procrastination but I can go to him for help to overcome it.

The first step to victory comes through facing up to the reasons why I procrastinate. Sometimes, to be honest, it's laziness. Writing is hard work! It's easier to talk about it than to do it. But since I know writing is the work God has called me to do, I need to heed Romans 12:11 (TLB) and, "Never be lazy in [my] work but serve the Lord enthusiastically."

Sometimes I procrastinate because I'm overextended. I have difficulty saying "no." All too often my time and energy are drained as I allow my priorities to get out of order. And then there's the "tyranny of the urgent."* I find myself ruled by my never-ending "to-do" list that is filled with things that seem to demand my attention but have no eternal significance.

Other times I procrastinate because of a problem with my will. I know what God has called me to do, but I choose to do what *I* want. It's not easy for me to discipline myself to stay in my office when it's a beautiful day outside or when a friend calls and wants to chat. Even though I usually win that battle because I enjoy working, I still may not end up accomplishing what *God* wants me to do.

An editor gave me a go-ahead on a book proposal. I told him I would have the manuscript to him in three months. Then I began procrastinating! I told myself I could work more efficiently if I reorganized my files. Then I got side-tracked answering letters and reworking manuscripts that had been sitting around for months. That got me in the mood to market my returned manuscripts that really should, I convinced myself, get back out in the mail. Before I realized it, a month had passed without even five minutes spent on the book manuscript. Why? I procrastinate because I'm afraid of failure!

Facing the reasons why I procrastinate doesn't make me feel good, but it is a prerequisite to the second step to victory--confession. My good intentions are not enough. They do not get me "off the hook."

Jesus told a parable about a man with two sons (see Matt. 21:28-31). He asked both of them to go and work in the vineyard. The first son said he wouldn't, but later he changed his mind and did what his father asked. The second son said he would, but he didn't. He procrastinated!

When God calls something to my attention, it's not what I say I will do that counts--it's what I actually do because "knowing what is right to do and then not doing it [in other words, procrastinating] is sin" (James 4:17, TLB). It is only as I confess this sin and realize my worthlessness before the Lord, that he lifts me up, encourages, and helps me (see James 4:8-10). While some opportunities may be gone forever, God does not leave me in the land of regrets. He is able to redeem the time I've lost procrastinating and to give me "another chance" (see Prov. 28:13, TLB).

The third step to victory requires that I risk being open and honest with other Christians--especially writers. "Admit your faults to one another and pray for each other" James 5:16 (TLB) says. That's not an easy thing to do. Yet people cannot pray on-target for my needs, if they don't know what they are. It has been a tremendous help and encouragement to know that others are praying for me--and holding me accountable to do the things I've told them I feel called to do.

Other steps I have taken to try to overcome procrastination include: Memorizing Scripture promises, re-examining my priorities, and making lists. I have even used a system of rewards and punishments, "earning" the right to do the things I want to do, by doing *first* the thing I would prefer to put off. Some methods help. Others do not. But I am finding that the most important step after self-examination, confession, and seeking the prayer support of others, is such a simple one I often overlook it. At the beginning of each day I need to ask, "Lord, what do *you* want me to do?"

When I allow the Lord to be Lord of my schedule and my daily "to-do" list, I am less prone to procrastinate. Minute-by-minute obedience pleases God. It also frees me from the frustration of being torn in different directions by my unrealistic expectations and the resulting burden of guilt. As I leave my schedule to the Lord, he brings order to what would otherwise be chaos, and peace to what would otherwise be confusion.

God knows what needs to take priority in my life at any given moment. He shows me those priorities when I stop long enough to ask him and to wait for his response. He may remind me of promises I've made or tasks that I've put off that need to be done--today. But what he calls me to do, he also equips me to do. He never asks me to do the impossible.

As I'm learning to be obedient--to be a doer of his Word rather than a procrastinator--exciting things are happening. I'm discovering the joy of being used in his Kingdom work in ways I could have easily missed.

Responding to God's Call to Write

Ecclesiastes 3:1 (TLB) says, "There is a right time for everything." This may not be the right time for you to write. But if you have clearly felt God's call to write and you know you are procrastinating, you need to ask yourself:

1. Why do I procrastinate?

2. What ideas have I scribbled on a scrap of paper that I know I should be developing?

3. If I knew Jesus was coming back this week, or this month, or this year, what completed manuscript would I most want to lay at his feet?

* I highly recommend the booklet *Tyranny of the Urgent* by Charles H. Hummell (InterVarsity Press, 1971).

If you want to know what God wants you to do, ask him,
and he will gladly tell you....
James 1:5, TLB

7
Keeping in Balance

I love my in-laws. Yet when they visited, I could not relax. Instead, I found myself wishing I could sit down and get to work on an idea for an article. Without having to be told, I knew my work as a writer had again become too important and consuming. Once again it had gotten out of balance with my other priorities.

I knew God had called me to write. I also knew that unless I found a more balanced way to pursue my work as a writer, both I and my family would suffer. Although I had the self-discipline to work twelve-hour days, I was not any more fruitful than the writer who lacks discipline and works only sporadically. I was not producing quality material, nor was I giving my family--or anyone or anything else--quality time. My long hours created little more than physical, mental, emotional, and spiritual fatigue. I obviously had a lot to learn about prioritizing and keeping in balance.

The Bible says, "Fear God--know that He is, revere and worship Him --and keep His commandments" (Eccl. 12:13, AMP). In the midst of my busyness serving God, I had forgotten the importance of my relationship with him and with others. I had given too high a priority to my work and put an unbalanced emphasis on Romans 12:11 (TLB): "Never be lazy in your work but serve the Lord enthusiastically."

Because writing is work, and work that must be done in God's way if we want God's blessing, it is important to periodically assess the way we approach our work as writers. Is the effectiveness of our writing ministry being hindered because we are inclined to overwork? Does our writing consume too much of our time and energy? Or, is our problem one of spending too little time writing? With multiple demands on our time, how can we order our priorities and keep our lives in balance?

My writing mentor gave me some valuable insights. "Life is like a table with four legs," she said. "If any one of those legs is too long or too short, the table is wobbly."

"And my work as a writer is just one of those legs," I observed, "yet I've allowed it to unbalance my whole life." Out of our conversation came the decision to make the time to pray in depth--not just about my writing, but about my entire life.

First of all, I acknowledged that my table, my life, had to rest on God and his Word. My faith couldn't be one of the legs--it had to be the foundation. My relationship with God had to permeate every area of my life.

What about the legs of my table? The Lord showed me three others, besides my writing, that I too often overlooked in my zeal to "write his answer."

My family, of course, is one of the legs. All the help my writing might provide to others will be worth nothing if I fail my own family. My responsibility as a wife and mother is more than just doing things *for* them; it is doing things *with* them. I must guard against my tendency to become preoccupied with my work, and must make a conscious decision to be there for them--to give them my full attention and to really listen to what they are saying (and not saying).

Extended family, friends, and even strangers are another one of the legs. God reminded me that my life will never be in balance if I become a hermit. I cannot allow my response to the Great Commission to be only that of writing words to a faceless audience. I also have something to give people face-to-face, and they have something to give me. The joy of developing and strengthening close relationships is one I must not sacrifice to sitting alone before my computer for endless hours.

Finally, I saw that the last leg, but not the least, is myself. "Perhaps it's time to learn again that the entire world doesn't rest on your shoulders, and that recreation--think of it as re-creation--is also part of God's plan," another wise friend counseled me.

I knew she was right. I need time for myself--for things I enjoy doing, other than work. I cannot expect to be whole, or to write anything to help others become whole, if I never have any time just for me. While my children often play too much, all too frequently my life gets so out of balance that I don't play at all.

I am still following the proverb that says, "Commit your work to the Lord, then it will succeed" (Prov. 16:3, TLB), but I'm learning that does not mean I need to be a superwoman. I'm finding *The Living Bible's* paraphrase of Philippians 4:13 helpful: "I can do everything *God asks me to* with the help of Christ who gives me the strength and power" (italics added). As I listen, really listen, for his instructions, he helps me to keep in balance.

Responding to God's Call to Write

Is my writing in the proper balance with the rest of my priorities?

Which legs make up the table of my life?

What one specific thing can I do today to get, or to stay, in balance?

God, help me to understand what you want me to do today,
make me wise about spiritual things,
and help me to live this day
in a way that will please and honor you.
Colossians 1:9-10, author's paraphrase

Be still before the Lord and wait patiently for him....
Psalm 37:7, NIV

8
Learning to Wait

"Oh no," I groaned as I picked up my mail. My book manuscript had been returned--for the fourth time. The news at the typewriter repair shop wasn't any better. My typewriter was obsolete and couldn't be repaired. We couldn't afford to replace it. *At least I've got a week to figure out what to do,* I told myself as I packed for a much-needed vacation.

Our vacation flew by with no clear direction from the Lord. I knew he was still calling me to write, but he didn't give me any answers for my present dilemma. When I got home, things went from bad to worse. I was greeted with a bundle of mail that contained *twenty-one* returned manuscripts--including the story I had hoped would get me to the *Guideposts* Writer's Workshop.

"Oh Lord," I sighed. "I'm tired of trying and yet failing, of waiting and hoping, only to be disappointed."

Choosing to ignore the advice I readily give others--don't waste time feeling sorry for yourself but get those manuscripts back in the mail and then get to work on a new idea--I walked out of my office, slamming the door behind me. As I was fixing myself a snack in the kitchen (something else I shouldn't have been doing), I felt the Lord's presence and his unmistakable voice speaking to me within.

"The lessons I'm trying to teach you, my child, are more important than the sale of hundreds of manuscripts."

"But Lord," I began to object, as I often do.

"Peace. Be still," he said firmly.

In an unexplainable way, the churning within me ceased. I knew he was going to show me something important.

"I want you to learn to wait patiently, productively, and expectantly," he said.

I pondered those words the rest of the day. The productive and expectant part sounded okay, but I had trouble with the patience part. So, I realized, did a lot of others--even the patriarchs of Scripture.

At age seventy-five Abram left his people and his land. "'Go into the land I will guide you to. If you do,'" God promised, "'I will cause you to become the father of a great nation'" (Gen. 12:1-2, TLB). The Bible doesn't tell us how long it took Abram to reach Canaan, but traveling on foot with his flocks and entire household, it certainly wasn't an overnight journey. The fulfillment of the other part of the promise took twenty-five years of waiting and wondering. After all, his wife was barren and wasn't getting younger. But even though she ran ahead of the Lord and created a legacy of problems that still exist today, God, in his perfect timing, honored his promise and blessed them with a son.

I thought of Jacob, waiting and working fourteen years for Rachel to be his wife, and the years the people of Israel waited for God to free them from slavery in Egypt. And then there were the forty years of wandering when it must have seemed like they would never reach the Promised Land.

It's a question of whether or not I trust the Lord and his timing, I admitted. Do I really believe that he knows the plans he has for me, that they are plans for good and not for evil, to give me a future and a hope (see Jer. 29:11, TLB)? If God's people in Babylonian captivity believed this promise, why couldn't I? How much more confirmation did I need that God was calling me to write? But, as always, I wanted him to make things happen quickly and easily. Then I saw in a new way how God did not shorten the time of waiting even for the birth of his Son.

How difficult those nine months must have been for Mary. First there was the fear of whether or not Joseph would believe her story. If he chose not to, she knew he could accuse her of adultery. The penalty would have been death by stoning.

Even when God intervened and assured Joseph that the child had been conceived by the Holy Spirit, Mary still had to face the wagging tongues of the townspeople. I can imagine the pain she must have experienced daily as she went to the well and was ostracized by women who had once been her friends. And there was the very real and difficult wait of those last weeks--the uncomfortable and long journey to Bethlehem on a donkey, the wait to find a place to stay, and the hours of labor.

I wondered what lessons Mary learned during that time. Were they ones that prepared her to face her Son's death on a cross? Certainly the lesson of patience--of trusting the Lord to bring about all he had promised --must have been one of the lessons. I also suspect that she learned to use those months productively, preparing in practical ways for the birth and care of her Son. And throughout that time of waiting, there was undoubtedly a thread of expectancy--of awe that God was permitting her to be a part of his plan.

There are parallels for myself and my work as a writer. If I fail to learn the lesson of patience, I won't be prepared to persist during other dry spells. The challenge Lee Roddy once gave me to, "Write so that heaven will be different," will never happen if my lack of patience makes me become a quitter.

If I choose to use waiting times to indulge in self-pity--to spend hours on the phone griping to other writers about "those editors," time that could be used productively will be lost.

And finally, failing to learn to wait expectantly will be the denial of a Scripture I promised years ago to heed: "I will keep on expecting you to help me. I praise you more and more....I walk in the strength of the Lord God" (Ps. 71:14,16, TLB)--through the times when my writing is bearing fruit, as well as through the times when I must wait for it to mature and ripen.

Responding to God's Call to Write

If your writing ministry seems to be "on hold," ask the Lord, "What are you trying to teach me?" Be still in his presence. Write his answer here.

Think of specific things you can do to wait patiently, productively, and expectantly.

Read the following Scriptures. Which passage most directly speaks to your need today? Begin the process of memorizing it by writing it out below and on a card to post above your typewriter or word processor.

Psalm 27:14   Psalm 130:3-6

Psalm 32:8   Isaiah 40:29-31

Psalm 42:11   Hebrews 11:1

But O my soul, don't be discouraged.
Don't be upset. Expect God to act!
For I know that I shall again have plenty of reason
to praise him for all that he will do....
Psalm 42:11, TLB

9
In Dry Times

"I'll never run out of ideas," I've often said. With a file drawer full of notes and manuscripts in various stages of completion, I felt certain that the periods of dryness, or writer's block, which I heard other writers complain about, would not affect me. But then something happened to me that was far worse. I felt empty inside!

The evil one began to fill me with doubts. "You so often fail to live as a Christian," he hissed, "how can you expect to help others? You're nothing but a hypocrite. You should give up writing."

Every time I sat down at my desk, I got a tension headache. Increasingly I began to dread facing the work I always loved to do. "Maybe it is time to quit," I said to my husband one evening. "I'm willing to work hard and to face rejection, but if I no longer have anything to share..."

Paul put his arms around me. "You'll feel inspired again. I know you will."

"But what if God doesn't want me to write anymore?"

The phone rang. It was an editor at David C. Cook asking me to write a series of devotionals. My heart pounded with excitement. A Sunday evening phone call from an editor, right after I had questioned my call... It couldn't be a coincidence! I thanked God for showing me that my writing ministry wasn't over.

With new enthusiasm I sat down at my typewriter the next morning, but still I felt empty. Ideas wouldn't flow. I turned to the discouraging task of resubmitting manuscripts. As I plodded along, the whispers grew more intense. "You're a failure. You don't have what it takes. God can't use you."

I couldn't get to sleep that night. I tried praying, but God seemed distant. Suddenly I remembered something Lee Roddy told me when I was struggling to complete my first book. "You're listening to the wrong voice, Marlene," he said.

The burden began to lift as I thought of Lee's words and the Scriptures that point to Satan as the father of lies. He is the Christian writer's great adversary. He is intent on destroying our writing ministries, our homes, our very lives.

"But God," I prayed, "it's sometimes so hard to discern your voice. The enemy's whispers often seem so true. I do fail to respond to situations in Christlike ways--to practice what I preach. It's easy to believe that makes me unworthy to share your Word."

"Condemnation is the work of the evil one," God reminded me. "My Spirit brings conviction of sin and the strength to overcome it. I know you're not perfect. None of the people I use are perfect. They are *willing* people. Are you still willing, child?"

"Oh yes, Lord," I said as I fervently prayed that I would again experience the anointing of his Spirit. "Please speak to me so that I can write the words you want me to write."

The next day my writer's block lifted. Sentences began to flow--not in perfect form or structure--but then that never has been my experience. I always spend a lot of time rewriting and editing. But, praise God, I again had words to rewrite and edit!

Since then I've experienced other times of dryness. They seem almost cyclical, like the droughts that periodically occur in nature. But I'm learning that God allows these times in my life to teach me valuable lessons about the importance of letting my roots grow down into him (see Col. 2:7). I'm also learning to follow his drought emergency instructions in James 4:6-10:

1. Humble yourself before the Lord and ask him to remove any false pride (see James 4:6). Affirm anew that he is the Source of your creativity.

2. "Submit yourselves, then, to God" (James 4:7, NIV). *The NIV Interlinear Greek-English New Testament* reads: "Be ye subject therefore to God." According to *Vine's Expository Dictionary of New Testament Words,* the Greek word for "subject," *hupotasso,* is "primarily a military term, to rank under." We need to remember that God is not our buddy or our errand boy. Rather, "all things were created by him and for him. He is before all things, and in him all things hold together. And he is the head of the body, the church..." (Col. 1:16-18, NIV).

3. "Resist the devil" (James 4:7, NIV). Put on the helmet of salvation to protect your mind from the evil one's accusations. Pick up the shield of faith to "extinguish all the flaming arrows of the evil one" (Eph. 6:16, NIV).

4. "Come near to God" (James 4:8, NIV). Whether you feel his presence or not, spend an increased amount of time in prayer and in his Word. To stop your mind from wandering, pray aloud or write down your prayers. You might also want to read Scripture aloud. Grab hold of the promise: "Forever, O Lord, your Word stands firm in heaven. Your faithfulness extends to every generation, like the earth you created; it endures by your decree, for everything serves your plans" (Ps. 119:89-91, TLB).

5. "Grieve, mourn and wail" (James 4:9, NIV) over the ways you fail the Lord. Ask him to make you a cleansed vessel through which his power can flow.

6. "Realize your worthlessness before the Lord" and allow him to "lift you up, encourage and help you" (James 4:10, TLB).

I praise God for the way "he lifted me out of the pit of despair, out from the bog and the mire, and set my feet on a hard, firm path and steadied me as I walked along. He has given me a new song to sing, of praises to our God. Now many will hear of the glorious things he did for me, and stand in awe before the Lord, and put their trust in him" (Ps. 40:2-3, TLB).

Responding to God's Call to Write

Expand on the above drought emergency instructions by using a concordance to find and list below passages about humility, submission, and God's sovereignty. Praise him for the privilege he has given you to be used in his Kingdom work.

I am still not all I should be....
Philippians 3:13, TLB

10
Be Honest

"Write about what you know." We've heard it over and over, but it's true. Our best writing will grow out of our personal experiences. Reading through Acts and the letters of the apostle Paul, it's obvious Paul recognized the importance of being open, honest, and vulnerable.

"I am still not all I should be," Paul admitted to the Christians in Philippi (Phil. 3:13, TLB). How important it is to communicate this to our readers! If we feel we have arrived, we will talk down to them or preach at them and they won't read beyond the first paragraph. But if we are honest about our struggles and failures, they will be able to identify with us and will want to read on.

Sometimes it isn't easy to be honest with ourselves, much less with others. Our past may be too painful to remember or to share. Our present may be filled with things we don't want to think about, much less write about. Yet, if we're going to write for the Lord, we need to be willing to open our lives to others. We need to learn, like Paul did, to use our personal experiences to glorify the Lord Jesus Christ and to lead others to him.

Acts 8:3 (TLB) says that, before his conversion, "Paul was like a wild man, going everywhere to devastate the believers, even entering private homes and dragging out men and women alike and jailing them." Even though Paul knew the Lord had forgiven him, it still must have grieved him to remember the pain he inflicted on those who were now fellow believers.

For years Paul chafed under the distrust of the church leaders. Despite the later success of his missionary tours and all the suffering he endured for the cause of Christ, he was never totally accepted by some of the Jewish Christians.

It would have been natural and understandable for Paul to want to forget his past and even to try and hide it. Instead, in both his spoken and written testimony, he chose to be open and honest. Before a mob at the temple in Jerusalem, Paul admitted that he "persecuted the Christians, hounding them to death, binding and delivering both men and women to prison" (Acts 22:4, TLB). But then, he went on to describe how the Lord met him on the road to Damascus and dramatically changed his life.

"Even though I was once a blasphemer and a persecutor and a violent man," Paul later wrote to Timothy, "I was shown mercy...so that in me, the worst of sinners, Christ Jesus might display his unlimited patience as an example for those who would believe on him and receive eternal life" (1 Tim. 1:13,16, NIV).

We, too, need to share our witness of the ways Christ has changed us. Without our testimony, others may feel there is no hope for them. They may question how God can love them or how he can change them. If we are to "shine out among them like beacon lights" (Phil. 2:15, TLB), we must be willing to take off our masks and be real.

Again, we can learn from Paul's example of honesty and openness. He admitted that he didn't understand himself. "I really want to do what is right," he said, "but I can't. I do what I don't want to--what I hate" (Rom. 7:15, TLB). Yet out of his awareness of his own sinful nature, Paul was able to point others to the "power of the life-giving Spirit" (Rom. 8:2, TLB). We can do the same.

But what about the evil one's accusation that we have no business writing our testimony because we're not always living in victory? Once again we need to look to Paul. From prison in Rome he wrote to the Philippians: "I haven't learned all I should even yet, but I keep working toward that day when I will finally be all that Christ saved me for and wants me to be" (Phil. 3:12, TLB). It is not our goodness or our obedience to God's laws that will save us or our readers; rather it is the shed blood of Jesus Christ. We need to point our readers to the Cross, not to ourselves.

Finally, Paul realistically portrayed the difficulties involved in following Christ. "We are pressed on every side by troubles," he wrote, "but not crushed and broken. We are perplexed because we don't know why things happen as they do, but we don't give up and quit. We are hunted down, but God never abandons us. We get knocked down, but we get up again and keep going" (2 Cor. 4:8-9, TLB).

Paul's call to spread the Good News of Jesus Christ to the gentile world was not an easy one. He patiently endured "suffering and hardship and trouble of every kind" (2 Cor. 6:4, TLB), but these were the very things that made his words credible. He was able to "show" from his "personal experience" how God would also "tenderly comfort" his readers and give them the "strength to endure" (2 Cor. 1:6-7, TLB).

Just as Paul urged the early Christians to pattern their lives after his (see Phil. 3:17), I believe he would urge us to pattern our writing after his. With God's help we can, like Paul, write openly and honestly about our personal experiences in such a way that non-believers will be won to Christ and believers will be encouraged and strengthened.

Responding to God's Call to Write

1. Inventory the rough moments of your life. When were you most aware of God's presence? When did you grow the most? Make a written list.

2. Bring your list to the Lord and ask him to show you which experiences you are ready to write about. Be especially open to those that make you feel most vulnerable as they are likely to be the ones that will have the greatest impact on your readers. Write a brief prayer asking the Lord to help you bring glory to him through your testimony.

3. Write the promise of Philippians 4:13 in your own words and get to work.

"I chose you and appointed you
to go and bear fruit...."
John 15:16, NIV

11
Bearing Fruit

As I sit at my word processor this morning, I find myself looking out the window and daydreaming. It is a bitter cold February day. A winter storm has encrusted the trees and bushes with a thick layer of ice that glistens in the bright sunshine. Spring seems a long way off. Wistfully I dream of golden daffodils and fragrant lilacs.

My thoughts wander to the vegetable seeds I planted yesterday. How good it will be to have fresh, home-grown tomatoes, peppers, and cauliflower. But then the ringing of the phone brings me back to the present and, after a brief conversation, back to this blank screen. "Lord, what do you want to say through me?" I ask.

"Bear fruit," I feel him speak to my heart.

I sigh. For all my hard work this past month, I don't feel I have borne much fruit. January's mail was slow to bring acceptances or checks. As usual I am fighting discouragement and self-doubt. "I feel as if I've plowed and planted my garden, but nothing is growing," I complain to the Lord. "It's not that I mind the hard work. But when, Lord, am I going to see the fruit of my labors?"

"Have you forgotten what I taught you about abiding?" he replies.

I open my Bible to John 15:4 (TLB) and read: "'Take care to live in me, and let me live in you. For a branch can't produce fruit when severed from the vine. Nor can you be fruitful apart from me.'"

I think back over the past weeks and the many excuses I've made to short-change my quiet time with the Lord. It's no wonder my writing is not bearing fruit. I have been trying to do it in my strength instead of the Lord's.

Again, I feel the Lord remind me that my relationship *with* him is more important than anything I can do *for* him. Then, in a new way, I also see the kind of fruit he longs for me to bear. It isn't powerful prose or beautiful poetry, but rather the fruit of Christlikeness.

"But when the Holy Spirit controls our lives he will produce this kind of fruit in us: love, joy, peace, patience, kindness, goodness, faithfulness, gentleness and self-control," I read from Galatians 5:22-23 (TLB). To be honest, I have to admit that this fruit is sometimes sadly lacking in my life.

Love for the Lord and my readers is not always my motivating force. Far too often I am caught up in the ego trip of seeing my name in bigger and better magazines. And when editors do not accept my work, I do not feel very loving towards them.

My *joy* is lost when I push myself to get manuscripts in the mail and measure my fruitfulness by the number of acceptances I receive in return. My *peace* is destroyed when I take my focus off the Lord and put it on myself--on my goals, my needs, my feelings.

My *patience* wears thin when things don't happen as quickly as I want them to, or as quickly as I feel they should. Instead of waiting on God and his perfect timing, I become discouraged and irritable. I find myself saying unkind things to the people I love, especially to my children, when they interrupt me when I'm trying to write.

Goodness makes me think of Paul's words about Jesus: "He went around doing good" (Acts 10:38, TLB). Am I "doing good" through what I write? Using Lee Roddy's acrostic, *BERT,* do my words really *"Benefit"* my readers? Do they *"Enrich"* them? Are they *"Relevant"* and *"Timely"*?

Faithfulness. The Bible assures me that, "The one who calls [me] is faithful" (1 Thess. 5:24, NIV). Therefore, I do not have to become consumed by the dollars and hours part of my writing--by the little I earn for the long hours I work. Instead, I can choose to trust his promise to supply all my needs (see Phil. 4:19) and to remain faithful to my call to write his answer (see Hab. 2:2).

Gentleness, I learn as I look at the original Greek meaning of the word, is not just the way I treat others. *Vine's Expository Dictionary of New Testament Words* points out that it is better translated as *meekness* and is "closely linked with the word *tapeinophrosune* [humility], and...it is only the humble heart which is also the meek, and which, as such, does not fight against God and more or less struggle and contend with Him." Instead of almost demanding that God "bless" my ministry, I need to surrender my desires to him. I need to follow Jesus' example and remember how he took on "the very nature of a servant,...humbled himself and became obedient to death" (Phil. 2:7-8, NIV).

Self-control makes me think of discipline and my need to take control of the hours in each day, as well as my thoughts, feelings, and actions which often defeat me. I can choose not to dwell on the negatives and not to procrastinate. Most of all, daily, I can choose to relinquish control of my life to the Lord and trust him to work in me and through me.

"'Yes, I am the Vine; you are the branches,'" I feel him speak to me again through his Word. "'Whoever lives in me and I in him shall produce a large crop of fruit'" (John 15:5, TLB). He doesn't say *when,* but he also doesn't say *maybe.* Instead, he gives me the conditions. I must deliberately choose to abide in him. I must submit to his pruning of my motives and goals. I must take care to stay close to him--to let him live in me. Only then will my life and my words bear fruit.

Responding to God's Call to Write

Is the fruit of the Spirit evident in my life? Do I have:

Love?   Joy?

Peace?

Patience?

Kindness?

Goodness?

Faithfulness?

Gentleness?

Self-control?

"We don't know what to do, but we are looking to you."
2 Chronicles 20:12, TLB

12
Winning the Battle

Getting into print is like fighting a battle--a battle I was losing! During a recent writers' conference, three editors requested manuscripts and then returned them, crushing my hopes. The editor of a magazine I contribute to regularly sent back my latest submission with the note, "Sorry, but this wasn't one of your better ones." My mentor tore apart what I thought was one of the best pieces I'd ever written. An assignment wasn't coming together, but then I was too exhausted battling discouragement to have any energy left for writing.

I dumped my feelings on my husband, expecting him to be sympathetic as always. Instead he said, "You know this is part of what it means to be a writer. If you can't handle it, then quit."

"Quit? No!" I exclaimed.

"Then you need to heed the advice you give others." He reached out and hugged me. "Remember how you tell them they need to toughen up and keep praising the Lord?"

I sighed. I knew Paul was right. Like a little child who hadn't gotten her way, I had been pouting instead of praising. Silently I asked the Lord to forgive me and to show me how to win the battle. Later I felt him lead me to the story of King Jehoshaphat in 2 Chronicles 20.

Jehoshaphat is in a precarious position. The armies of Moab, Ammon, and the Meunites have declared war on him and the people of Judah. Jehoshaphat is "badly shaken" by the news that "'a vast army is marching'" against him (see verses 2-3, TLB). But he doesn't just stand there and wring his hands. He knows his nation needs God's help. He also knows they are not worthy to ask for it. Therefore, he sends out a proclamation that "all the people of Judah should go without food for a time, in penitence and intercession before God" (verse 3, TLB).

The Greater Philadelphia Christian Writers Fellowship that I lead has a prayer chain. I encourage our members to use it. Yet, even though I felt close to defeat, I failed to request their prayer support. I also failed to recognize my need to humble myself before the Lord and seek forgiveness for my sins (see James 4:7-10).

I can picture people from all over Judah crowding into the temple court. I can hear the hush as Jehoshaphat begins to lead them in prayer. "'O Lord God of our fathers--the only God in all the heavens, the Ruler of all the kingdoms of the earth--you are so powerful, so mighty. Who can stand against you?'" (verse 6, TLB).

I often forget to begin my prayers with praise. I tend to get right to the problem, as if God's time (and mine) is too valuable to waste with preliminaries. But how important these preliminaries are! I must never lose that sense of awe and wonder when I come into the presence of God. He is worthy of my praise, and it is the very act of praising him that changes my perspective and enables me to pray with power.

Jehoshaphat continues his prayer by focusing on all God has done in the past. My memory of God's faithfulness and his ability to use each problem, each trial, for my good is often very short.

"'O our God,...didn't you give this land forever to the descendants of your friend Abraham?'" Jehoshaphat reminds God (verse 7, TLB). God has made promises to me, too. I've underlined many of them in my Bible. I don't need to remind God of these promises. I need to remind myself.

"'We have no way to protect ourselves against this mighty army,'" Jehoshaphat admits. "'We don't know what to do, but we are looking to you'" (verse 12, TLB).

When I try to do things in my own strength, God does not intervene. It is only as I surrender the situation to him, as I admit that I am powerless, that I begin to experience his power flowing through me. Like Jehoshaphat, it is then I hear God say, "'The battle is not yours, but God's!...Don't be afraid or discouraged...for the Lord is with you!'" (verses 15,17, TLB).

When King Jehoshaphat heard these words, he fell with his face to the ground and worshipped the Lord. The next morning, in obedience to the Lord, the army of Judah went out to meet the enemy with a choir leading the way. As they began to sing and praise, the Lord caused the enemy to begin fighting among themselves. The army of Judah didn't have to strike a single blow!

During the battles that are a part of growing as a writer, how often do I praise the Lord *before* I win the victory? I don't mean just mouthing the words, but falling down before him and worshipping him? Despite circumstances that discourage me and make me feel like giving up, do I recognize his sovereignty and choose to serve him with a thankful heart and with "holy fear and awe" (Heb. 12:28, TLB)?

I'd like to tell you I consistently do these things, but I don't. The truth is, the more I come to know the Lord, the more I am aware of the many ways I fall short of what I should be. And yet God, in his mercy and grace, is allowing me to be used in his Kingdom work.

A month ago I taught at the Colorado Christian Writers Conference. I was weary from the spiritual attack I'd been under for weeks, but as I stood to speak, I again experienced God giving me the victory and the empowering of the Holy Spirit. The next day I spent a life-changing time alone with the Lord in the Rocky Mountains. As I drove the steep, winding road to the highest overlook, I felt like I was being drawn into the very presence of God.

"'For you are dealing with the one who formed the mountains and made the winds, and knows your every thought,'" God spoke to me through his Word (Amos 4:13, TLB).

Never have I been so aware of his holiness and my unworthiness. Eleven thousand feet above sea level, I knelt and worshipped him. I recommitted my life to the work he has called me to do and asked him to make me strong for the battles yet to come.

I've known the Lord for over a quarter of a century, and yet this was the first time I had ever spent such a large block of time alone with God, worshipping him and allowing him to refresh and renew me for the work he is calling me to do. I've resolved to make more time to worship him who is "'Holy, holy, holy, Lord God Almighty--the one who was, and is, and is to come'" (Rev. 4:8, TLB).

Responding to God's Call to Write

When I feel I'm under attack do I, like Jehoshaphat, go to the Lord and seek the support of prayer partners?

Do I humble myself before the Lord and seek forgiveness for the ways I have failed him?

Am I learning to focus on his greatness, to remember his promises, and to praise him *before* the battle is won?

How long has it been since I've really taken time to be alone with the Lord simply to worship him?

Plan a time, now, and put it down on your calendar. Find a place away from the pressures of your home and office; out-of-doors in the magnificence of God's creation, if at all possible.

And my God will meet all your needs....
Philippians 4:19, NIV

13
Seek First His Kingdom

"May the Lord bring a new joy in letting him carry the burden for you so that you do not feel the pressure to perform."

I blink in amazement at the letter from an editor I deeply respect. Her words are incredibly on target. How did she know the pressure I have been under due to financial problems and the way that pressure drives me to "perform" at my typewriter? I know for certain I haven't said anything to her. I'm not in the habit of sharing my financial needs with editors, even those who are good friends. Yet, somehow, she looked into my soul and saw the struggle that some days threatens to make me give up and quit.

God has called me to write. Neither I nor my husband question his call. I know Paul fully supports my choice to stay home and write. But I also know our financial obligations make my writing seem like an unaffordable luxury. If I put in the same number of hours at a "real" job, there would be no worry of how to pay for college for our two children or how to pay for the repairs our house desperately needs. And Paul would not have to work a second job delivering pizzas four nights a week.

It is as if I'm engaged in a tug of war between what I know I am supposed to be doing and the realities that make it seem unrealistic. I feel guilty staying home and writing when I see my children doing without some things I'd like to be able to give them. And then the doubts come. I wonder whether I am torturing myself with writing aspirations that are only pipedreams.

I'm sure I'm not alone in this struggle. In today's economy, most everyone who is seriously pursuing a writing ministry will have to consider the cost involved. The fact is that it takes more than just time and talent to be a successful writer. There is also the investment of money--for a typewriter or computer, for postage, supplies, conferences, books, magazines.... And there is no guarantee we will recoup our expenses, much less make a profit.

Most Christian writers will claim a loss for several years. Even when we get out of the red, it may be a long time (if ever) before we are making what we could in another profession. I've often wondered whether a doctor, lawyer, clerk, or mechanic would be willing to put in the same long hours for the amount of money I earn writing for Christian periodicals.

To be honest, I have to admit that sometimes I feel angry and resentful over the hard work and poor pay I receive as a freelance Christian writer. Sometimes the sacrifices seem too great and the rewards too small. But because my writing is also my livelihood (or needs to be), I can't ignore these very real feelings. Instead, I have to deal with them and gain victory over them.

I am reminded of Jesus' words about God and money in the Sermon on the Mount. Jesus knew the hardships his countrymen endured because of the heavy taxes Rome imposed. When crops failed or the nets were empty, many of them went hungry. Yet, Jesus told them not to worry about food, drink, or clothes. He sought to change their perspective--to help them see that they should be grateful for life itself.

Jesus drew their attention to the birds of the air. "'They don't worry about what to eat--they don't need to sow or reap or store up food--for your heavenly Father feeds them. And'" he reminded them, "'you are far more valuable to him than they are'" (Matt. 6:26, TLB).

He pointed to the lilies in the field. "'King Solomon in all his glory was not clothed as beautifully as they'" (Matt. 6:29, TLB). Again he spoke words of reassurance, "'And if God cares so wonderfully for flowers that are here today and gone tomorrow, won't he more surely care for you, O men of little faith?'" (Matt. 6:30, TLB).

His words convict me. My faith is little. My perspective is wrong. Although God promises to meet all my needs, I waste a tremendous amount of emotional energy worrying, and thus give Satan a dangerous foothold in my life. I allow him to rob me of the joy of writing when I embrace negative thinking patterns and my list of "have nots." As a result, more times than I want to admit, I really have been ready to give up. Because my work is not selling and ministering to people? No. But because what I earn from manuscript sales never seems to be enough.

Then I am reminded of something else Jesus said. "'But seek first his kingdom and his righteousness, and all these things will be given to you as well'" (Matt. 6:33, NIV).

That is the key! I need to keep my priorities in order--to keep my eyes on the Lord and the Kingdom work he is calling me to do. I cannot lose sight of my call by allowing my writing to get tangled up with my worry about our finances. I need to see God as our Source instead of trying to meet our needs myself through "producing" bigger and better manuscripts that will bring in larger and more frequent checks. I have been assuming a burden God never meant for me to carry instead of trusting him to provide.

"Lord, please forgive me and help me," I pray. "Forgive me for putting a price tag on the work I do for you. Forgive me for my worry and my desire for earthly rewards. Help me to see everything I do in light of eternity."

The sense of release, which my friend prayed I would discover, comes as cleansing tears flow down my cheeks. I feel the joy of the Lord as I give my worries to him and recommit my work to him.

I know I'll have to do this over and over again. Victory is rarely instantaneous and complete. But I also know I'm going in the right direction, because in a new way I'm seeking first his kingdom and his righteousness, regardless of the cost. The other things--my genuine needs --will be taken care of by the Lord in his perfect timing. I can trust him. So can you.

Responding to God's Call to Write

God doesn't call everyone to be a full-time writer, but he does call us to trust him and to walk in obedience. Are you trusting and obeying, or are you thinking "lack"--lack of money, time, ability, or anything else?

Why do you feel this way?

Read Philippians 4:19. Make a list of the needs that face you today and what Jesus Christ has done in your life in the past.

What, specifically, is God asking you to do today to show that you believe this promise?

*Show to others how God called you out of the darkness
into his wonderful light.*
1 Peter 2:9, TLB

14
Like Peter

I've often written about the apostle Paul. I identify with him! If there was an early Christian workaholic, it was Paul. Undaunted by opposition and persecution, he traveled throughout the Roman world spreading the Gospel. Even when he settled in one place, he filled every hour with preaching, teaching, and tentmaking. His mind and his hands were never idle!

I admire Paul, but I love Peter. In a special, beautiful way I see his feelings, and failings, in the pages of the New Testament and I feel close to him.

The first time Peter's words are recorded in the gospel of Luke (see 5:1-11), he makes himself transparent. He was washing his nets beside the seashore while Jesus preached nearby. Noticing the empty boats, Jesus stepped into one and asked Peter to push it out into the water. I can picture Peter forgetting the nets and listening to Jesus. When Jesus finished speaking, he instructed Peter to go into deeper water and let down the nets.

Logic told Peter this was foolish. They had worked hard all night and caught nothing. Daytime fishing was a waste of time, but he obeyed

Jesus. And what incredible results! The nets were so full they began to tear. Peter didn't stop to analyze what had happened or to see who might be watching. He fell down on his knees and said, "'Oh, sir, please leave us--I'm too much of a sinner for you to have around'" (Luke 5:8, TLB). When they got to shore, he left everything and followed Jesus.

From then on Peter stayed close to Jesus. He was always up front, directing the crowds and speaking for the other disciples. Was Peter simply a naturally gifted leader? I'm not so sure. I can't help but wonder if Peter was trying to prove himself. He may have thought the others (even those who were also fishermen) were more likely candidates for discipleship. John was a deep thinker. Andrew could relate to people. James had studied the law.

The more Peter tried, the more he failed. He walked on water, only to sink. He boasted of his loyalty to the Master, only to deny him. Yet, on the day of Pentecost, Peter was transformed from a coward into a Spirit-filled preacher and leader. Even before the mighty Sanhedrin, he stood his ground. "'We cannot stop telling about the wonderful things we saw Jesus do and heard him say'" (Acts 4:20, TLB).

What can Christian writers learn from Peter? First of all, I believe he shows us what must happen in our lives when we come face to face with Jesus Christ. Like Peter, we need to confess our sins, recognizing that Jesus "personally carried the load of our sins in his own body when he died on the cross, so that we can be finished with sin and live a good life from now on" (1 Pet. 2:24, TLB). If our words are to have credibility, our walk needs to match our talk.

Peter also shows us the importance of obedience--of being willing to leave what we are doing to follow Jesus into unknown situations. The "safe" thing would have been for Peter to stay on the fringes of Jesus' life and ministry. He could have continued with his fishing business and taken time off only when Jesus was in town. But Peter chose to risk everything and follow Jesus.

I'm not suggesting anyone quit their job and go into a full-time writing ministry. I believe few are called to make a living at writing. But we can ask him to help us give up some things we enjoy doing in order to make time for writing, and to help us openly write about our struggles so that we can minister to the needs of others.

"'Feed my sheep'" (John 21:17, NIV) Jesus told Peter after his resurrection. No doubt Peter was still reeling from his denial of Jesus. Three times Jesus gave Peter the opportunity to reaffirm his commitment, and three times he challenged Peter to feed his sheep. Again Peter obeyed. He learned to care for the flock "willingly, not grudgingly"--not for what he would "get out of it," but because he was "eager to serve the Lord" (1 Pet. 5:2, TLB). He encourages us to do the same and to "do it with all the strength and energy that God supplies" (1 Pet. 4:11, TLB).

We need to "be ready" to share our faith and to "do it in a gentle and respectful way" (1 Pet. 3:15, TLB). "Preach [write] as though God himself were speaking through you," Peter says (1 Pet. 4:11, TLB). "Be ready to suffer" (1 Pet. 4:1, TLB) but focus on the "wonderful joy ahead, even though the going is rough for a while down here" (1 Pet. 1:6, TLB).

Another lesson from Peter is the need to deal with our egos. We are to "serve each other with humble spirits" (1 Pet. 5:5, TLB). Our insecurities may drive us to get our names in print, but like Peter we must be willing to give "all honor to God, the God and Father of our Lord Jesus Christ; for it is his boundless mercy that has given us the privilege of being born again" (1 Pet. 1:3, TLB). We must desire to point others to Jesus, not to ourselves.

Peter provides a lot more practical help that has direct application to our lives as writers: "Be clear minded and self-controlled so that you can pray" (1 Pet. 4:7, NIV). "Keep on doing what is right and trust yourself to the God who made you, for he will never fail you" (1 Pet. 4:19, TLB). "Stand firmly in his love" (1 Pet. 5:12, TLB).

In 2 Peter 1:2-8 (TLB) he describes ways to "grow strong spiritually and become fruitful and useful to our Lord Jesus Christ." Why? It's a process! It was for him and will be for us. Like Peter, there will be times when we will fail. But he rose above his failures and we can, too!

At Bill Gothard's Institute in Basic Youth Conflicts, I received a button with the letters "PBPGINFWMY"--"Please be patient. God is not finished with me yet." We also need to be patient with ourselves. Our faith is going to be tested (see 1 Pet. 1:7). Sometimes it may be found wanting. But the amount of our faith (remember what Jesus said about faith the size of a mustard seed?) is not as important as the One we believe in. Truly, he will "'never disappoint those who trust in him'" (1 Pet. 2:6, TLB). He has chosen us and he will equip us so that, through the words we write and the lives we live, we will "show to others how God called [us] out of the darkness into his wonderful light" (1 Pet. 2:9, TLB).

Responding to God's Call to Write

Read 1 and 2 Peter. Note below those passages that specifically speak to you and to your call to feed the flock of God through your writing. Commit one verse to memory today and ask God to work it into the fabric of your life.

Because the Lord God helps me, I will not be dismayed....
Isaiah 50:7, TLB

15
Disappointed But Not Discouraged

Six returns in one day! It isn't the first time, and I know it won't be the last. I handle it better now than I did when I was a beginning writer, yet it still hurts.

My writing is so much a part of me. It's hard not to view the return of a manuscript as a personal rejection. It's also hard not to question the Lord. I sought his Spirit's help as I wrote those pieces. I invested time, energy, and hard work. I know if I don't do something quickly the deadly D's are going to defeat me--disappointment, discouragement, doubt, and despair.

Then I feel God speak to me through his Word: "Since future victory is sure, be strong and steady, always abounding in the Lord's work, for you know that nothing you do for the Lord is ever wasted as it would be if there were no resurrection" (1 Cor. 15:58, TLB).

My thoughts turn to Jesus and how "he was willing to die a shameful death on the cross because of the joy he knew would be his afterwards" (Heb. 12:2, TLB). As the poster over my word processor says, "The answer lies in Christ." He wants to be my "leader and instructor" (Heb. 12:2, TLB). This can happen only if I choose to keep my eyes on him and not on the disappointments that threaten to discourage and defeat me.

I think of the disappointments Jesus faced. The poignancy of the opening lines of John's gospel again stir me: "Even in his own land and among his own people, the Jews, he was not accepted. Only a few would welcome and receive him" (John 1:11, TLB).

Jesus knew firsthand the pain of rejection! He was misunderstood and ridiculed even by his own brothers (see John 7:2-5). He endured the criticism of the religious leaders and the ostracism of those who felt nothing good could come from Nazareth (see John 1:46). And even in Nazareth, those who had known him since childhood refused to believe in him. Jesus' disappointment and hurt is evident in Mark's words: "And he could hardly accept the fact that they wouldn't believe in him" (Mark 6:6, TLB).

Jesus must have been even more disappointed at that point in his ministry when "many of his disciples turned away and deserted him" (John 6:66, TLB). I can only imagine how he must have felt as he turned to the Twelve and asked, "'Are you going too?'" (John 6:67, TLB). I wonder if the others nodded in agreement when Peter said, "'Master, to whom shall we go? You alone have the words that give eternal life, and we believe them and know you are the holy Son of God'" (John 6:68-69, TLB). Or, I wonder if some of them harbored unspoken doubts--especially as Jesus began to speak more and more of his death? One thing is certain. Jesus knew their thoughts. He knew that Peter would deny him, Judas would betray him, and that all of them would desert him.

"Father, strengthen me," I can imagine Jesus might have prayed. "Help me to rise above my feelings. Don't let the pain and disappointment I feel cause me to give up the work you have sent me to do. Don't let me succumb to discouragement."

While, of course, I do not know what Jesus prayed, I have no doubt that it was through those times alone with his Father that he received the strength he needed to overcome disappointments that make mine seem small in comparison. I also have no doubt that Jesus was a realist. He didn't set himself up for disappointment by putting his trust in men for "he knew mankind to the core. No one needed to tell him how changeable human nature is!" (John 2:24-25, TLB).

I believe the Parable of the Sower (see Luke 8:5-15) is Jesus' statement of faith and purpose. He is the Sower, the One who chose to come to earth and spread the seed that yields eternal life for all who believe. Like the farmer who works hard with no guarantee of a bounteous harvest, Jesus knows that not all of the seed sown will take root and grow to maturity. Some seed falls on hard soil--on indifferent hearts. Because they do not allow his Word to penetrate their hearts, Satan is able to snatch it away. Other seed falls on rocky soil--on those whose lives have little spiritual depth. They follow only as long as it is the easy thing to do. Still other seed falls on thorny ground--on those who are more interested in the things of the world than in seeking first his kingdom. But some seed falls on good soil. It takes root and produces a plentiful harvest that is worth the price of death on the cross.

I can hear Jesus speaking to me through this parable. "Be realistic. You can't expect, even with my help, to sell everything you write--certainly not the first time out. Maybe not even the tenth! It takes time and experience to learn to sow your seed effectively. It takes patience to wait while it grows to maturity. It takes faith to learn how to handle disappointment and not become discouraged. These lessons cannot be side-stepped if you want a writing ministry."

And I can also hear Jesus' words of warning. I cannot allow disappointments to beat me down so that I become like the hard soil. If I do, the evil one will be waiting to fill me with discouragement and to snatch away my joy and enthusiasm. I cannot become like the stony ground--someone who enjoys going to writing conferences and being challenged to write, but fails to go home and do it. Instead, I must make the decision to be productive by deliberately choosing to let my roots "grow down into him and draw up nourishment from him" (Col. 2:7, TLB).

I must be willing to pull out all the thorns, all those things that would distract me from wholeheartedly pursuing my call to write. And I must trust that in God's perfect timing, his words which have taken root in me, will be put onto paper and published so that he can use them to make a difference in the world. My life and my writing will produce a large crop of fruit if I hear the Word, retain it, and persevere (see Luke 8:15, NIV).

Responding to God's Call to Write

Read through one of the Gospels. Make a list of the situations that could have caused Jesus to feel disappointed and discouraged. Note how he handled each situation.

One of the best ways to deal with disappointments is to get your eyes off yourself and onto someone else--specifically onto the hopes, goals, and needs of other writers. Ask yourself: Do I know someone who shows promise as a writer--someone who could be, or should be, writing? Do I know a beginning writer I can nurture, or a struggling writer I can encourage? Write their names below. Begin to pray for them. Ask God to show you how he wants you to reach out to them.

Make the most of your chances to tell others the Good News.
Colossians 4:5, TLB

16
Prepare the Way

Will this be the year, month, week, or even the day when Jesus returns? He tells us to "'stay awake and be prepared'" (Matt. 25:13, TLB). That involves more than just sitting and observing "the signs of the times." As Christian writers, we have the privilege and responsibility to wait actively, pointing to those signs and presenting Christ's life alternative to our hurting world. We share with John the Baptist the task of preparing the way for Christ's coming.

This work of preparation must begin on a personal level. Like John, we need to be doing specific things in order to become the most effective communicators of God's truth. John didn't just stumble into his ministry as a forerunner. He prepared himself! He lived alone in the wilderness. He wore clothes woven from camel hair and a leather belt. He ate locusts and wild honey (see Mark 1:4,6).

I'm not suggesting that we leave our homes and families and move to some desolate spot. Nor am I suggesting we throw out our wardrobes and go on a fad diet. I know I couldn't eat a locust! But we do need to give some prayerful thought to John's example of preparation.

John gave top priority to spending time with the Lord and listening to his voice. He knew it was essential that he keep a servant's heart and that he not lose sight of his call to point to the Christ. "'He must become greater; I must become less,'" he said (John 3:30, NIV). How much time have we committed to being with the Lord, to listening to him, and to making certain our actions are in line with his will for our life?

John lived a very simple lifestyle. What steps are we taking to free ourselves from the clutter of things and activities in order to respond to God's call to write?

John ate natural foods. He took care of his health. Have we examined our eating habits and made up our minds to make needed changes? When are we going to start getting the exercise we need? Our bodies are the temple of God's Holy Spirit. He expects us to take care of them.

What was John's message? Isaiah foretold that he would be "a voice shouting from the barren wilderness, 'Prepare a road for the Lord to travel on! Widen the pathway before him!'" (Luke 3:4, TLB).

Having prepared ourselves--daily--for the ministry of writing, we need, in faith, to see that ministry widening and expanding. It's time to take the limits off God! If he is calling you to write a book, you need to write it. If you've had some work published but lately you've gotten lazy, you need to recommit yourself to your writing ministry, prayerfully set some measurable goals, and get to work.

If you're a beginner and you're reluctant to submit that first manuscript, perhaps you need to find the courage to read it to a critique group. Then you should take a leap of faith and mail it. It will never touch anyone from your desk drawer. If you know you need to learn more, join a workshop, go to a conference, take a creative writing class, or enroll in a correspondence school. But do something! Make room in your heart and life for the work he is calling you to do. Widen that pathway!

"'Level the mountains! Fill up the valleys! Straighten the curves! Smooth out the ruts!'" (Luke 3:5, TLB). This speaks to me about the need for maturity.

Our work as writers cannot be ruled by the ups and downs of our feelings. Beyond every mountaintop is another valley. Some days our writing efforts will seem futile. But God encourages us to "stand firm" on legs that are often shaky and to "mark out a straight, smooth path" for our feet (Heb. 12:12-13, TLB).

He calls us to follow him over the mountains and through the valleys --to stay on that narrow road that leads to life (see Matt. 7:14). He challenges us to walk in obedience and to watch out for the ruts along the way that can so easily cause us to stumble. The ruts are different for each one of us. For me they are the bad habits I keep falling into that limit my effectiveness and cause me to become discouraged. I need to look before I step. With his help, I can walk around that negative thought, the telephone, procrastination....

It takes hard work to conquer bad habits, to walk in obedience, to prepare the way for Christ's return. Weariness, frustration, and discouragement can become troublesome traveling companions. They certainly must have been for John. Repeatedly he was grilled by representatives of the "top pops" in Jerusalem. They wanted to know if he was the Messiah, or Elijah, or the Prophet. When he answered "no," they wanted to know what "right" he had to baptize (see John 1:19-27). But John boldly continued preaching.

John's call to repentance infuriated those who thought they were righteous. Eventually John's honesty and unwillingness to compromise his message led to his arrest. But even in prison, John was not bound by chains. He had a vision! He knew that one day "'all mankind shall see the Savior sent from God'" (Luke 3:6, TLB).

The writer of the book of Proverbs said, "Where there is no vision, the people perish" (Prov. 29:18, KJV). Our work as writers will also perish if we have no vision.

We should ask the Lord to open our eyes to the needs of people around us. Many are facing problems that seem like mountains. Their valleys are so deep they may turn to alcohol or drugs. Others, even teenagers, may try to take their lives. Some will succeed. But we can write words that will point them to the One who can heal their hurt and enable them to cope with life.

He is coming! When he comes I want to be doing the work he has called me to do. I want to be making the most of every chance I have to share the Good News (see Col. 4:5).

I praise God that each new day brings opportunities to serve him. I challenge you to catch a vision for the work he is calling *you* to do. Commit yourself to it--to him--and trust in his promises. Today is the day to begin preparing the way! Trust him to "make the darkness bright before [you] and smooth and straighten out the road ahead" (Isa. 42:16, TLB).

Responding to God's Call to Write

In the words of Dennis Rainey, National Director of Family Ministry, Campus Crusade for Christ, "Do you believe that God can give you a vision for your world that will capture you for the rest of your life?... What are you uniquely burdened for? What injustice causes you to pound the table and weep?"

Do you really believe God can use you to address these issues? Why or why not?

Claim Ephesians 3:20 and get to work *today* on that manuscript you want most to be able to lay at Jesus' feet when he returns.

"Cease striving and know that I am God...."
Psalm 46:10, NASB

17
Burnout!

Burnout--The New World Dictionary defines it: "To exhaust yourself by too much work." Having gone through several periods of burnout, my definition is much stronger. For me it is a state of being totally depleted --physically, mentally, emotionally, and spiritually. It is frightening and frustrating, especially since I know (and have used) the argument that claims Christians need not be victims of burnout because of the power of prayer and the availability of God's help.

Definitions and arguments aside, it is possible that each of us, no matter how deep our faith, will experience burnout at some point in our lives. It is not a state peculiar to writers; rather it is the product of the pressure and stress of daily living--the accumulation of problems and a never ending "to-do list" that causes both writers and non-writers to push themselves beyond their resources.

I vividly remember one time of burnout. I couldn't change the due dates of two assignments or the job I contracted to do for my husband's office just because I had gotten behind schedule. I also couldn't change the date of my daughter's graduation from high school or my in-law's visit. The awareness that I should have been more realistic in my planning might help in the future, but it wouldn't change things this time.

Although I was far from rested and ready for a writers' conference the following week, I couldn't postpone it or suddenly resign from the staff position I had accepted earlier. After five days of editing the conference newsletter, commuting, sleepless nights, and a tension headache, I was wiped out.

For most writers, conferences are a high--a time of inspiration and fresh resolve to pursue the call to write. For me, this conference was a bottoming-out experience. The one workshop I managed to squeeze in only made me realize how much I still needed to learn. I felt overwhelmed and inadequate. The road to becoming a successful writer was too much of an uphill climb. "It's just too hard, Lord," I cried. "I can't keep trying so hard, hoping so much, and being disappointed so greatly."

"Tell me," I blurted to an editor I bumped into after the closing program, "Do I really have what it takes? Will I ever reach my goals?"

She reminded me of my successes to date and how far I had come. "You're just tired," she said gently.

Embarrassed by my outburst and tears, I ran to my car. I started home, but I couldn't see the road. I pulled over and put my head on the steering wheel. Suddenly I remembered the story of Elijah. He had won an incredible victory over the prophets of Baal, but then he went from the mountaintop to the valley--actually the pit--of self-pity and depression. "'I've had enough,' he told the Lord" (1 Kings 19:4, TLB).

Like Elijah, I, too, had won some victories. God had given me the strength to accomplish what I needed to do. But then I lowered my shield of faith because my arms were too weary to hold it up. As a result, I became vulnerable to an avalanche of self-doubts.

A Scripture promise I memorized a long time ago came to mind: "He gives power to the tired and worn out, and strength to the weak....But they that wait upon the Lord shall renew their strength. They shall mount up with wings like eagles; they shall run and not be weary; they shall walk and not faint" (Isa. 40:29,31, TLB).

I didn't do much running or walking, much less writing, for weeks. I did, however, do a lot of learning and growing as I continued to reflect on Elijah's experience (see 1 Kings 19:1-18).

Someone has said that the difference between despair and hope is a good night's sleep. The first thing Elijah did was sleep. I needed some naps during the day as well--something I had never done.

After Elijah rested, an angel wakened him and told him to get up and eat. I realized how careless I had become about my eating habits. The food I grabbed on the run was too high in fats and carbohydrates. I knew I had been taking too great a risk with my problem of borderline low blood sugar.

Resting and eating sensibly helped me to gain a new perspective on things. I saw how I had been driving myself. When I did reach a goal, instead of stopping to rest (and to celebrate), I immediately got to work on my next project.

"With all the success you have had, there's always that note of it not being enough," someone I never met said to me in a letter. She read my column in *The Christian Writer* but probably would not have written to me if an editor had not mistakenly enclosed one of my manuscripts along with hers. She went on to say, "I have to constantly turn my goals and my eagerness and my frustrations over to the Lord, knowing that it is he who put this desire in me, but he doesn't want me to be a slave to it." I knew her letter and its timing was not a coincidence. It was a God-incident to get my attention.

In *Hearing God* (Baker Book House, 1988), Peter Lord observes that "Jesus' most-repeated statement (fifteen times in the New Testament) was: 'He that hath ears to hear, let him hear!'" God desires to speak to us but he won't shout to get our attention. As Elijah learned, God speaks not in the windstorm, the earthquake, or the fire, but in a gentle whisper (see 1 Kings 19:11-12). We can all too easily miss those whispers when we're striving, and driving ourselves, to reach our goals.

As we learn to rest in him, to listen to him, and to allow his mighty power to work within us, he will do "far more than we would ever dare to ask or even dream of--infinitely beyond our highest prayers, desires, thoughts, or hopes" (Eph. 3:20, TLB). But it will be in his timing, his way, and for his glory.

Responding to God's Call to Write

King David, the writer of Psalm 37, knew what it meant to strive, but he also knew how to "Rest in the Lord; wait patiently for him to act" (Ps. 37:7, TLB). Prayerfully read this psalm, asking God to speak to you regarding your own need to rest in him. Use the space that follows to write down those verses that challenge or convict you to make changes in your life.

"He has sent me to proclaim freedom...."
Luke 4:18, NIV

18
Proclaim Freedom

It was the first Independence Day! Rising to his feet in his home town synagogue, Jesus was handed the book of the prophet Isaiah. He began to read: "'The spirit of the Lord is upon me; he has appointed me to preach Good News to the poor; he has sent me to heal the broken-hearted and to announce that captives shall be released and the blind shall see, that the downtrodden shall be freed from their oppressors, and that God is ready to give blessings to all who come to him'" (Luke 4:18-19, TLB).

I can imagine how every eye was riveted on him as he added: "'These Scriptures came true today!'" (Luke 4:21, TLB).

There were no fireworks or hurrahs. Instead, they began to whisper among themselves.

"Isn't this Joseph's son?" someone must have asked.

"But he's so eloquent and wise."

"I heard he's been working miracles in Capernaum."

"How can that be? We've known him all his life."

"Yes, who does he think he is!"

"I solemnly declare to you," Jesus said, "that no prophet is accepted in his own home town! For example, remember how Elijah the prophet used a miracle to help the widow of Zarephath--a foreigner from the land of Sidon. There were many Jewish widows needing help in those days of famine....Or think of the prophet Elisha, who healed Naaman, a Syrian, rather than the many Jewish lepers needing help" (Luke 4:24-27, TLB).

His remarks infuriated them. As William Barclay says in his commentary on *The Gospel of Luke* (The Westminster Press, 1975), "The Jews were so sure that they were God's people that they utterly despised all others.... And here was this young Jesus, whom they all knew, preaching as if the *gentiles* were specially favoured by God." They mobbed him and took him to the edge of the hill on which the city was built. They were ready to push him over the cliff, but Jesus "walked away through the crowd and left them" (Luke 4:30, TLB).

Mark's account says Jesus "could hardly accept the fact that they wouldn't believe in him" (6:6, TLB). I can feel his disappointment, but I also feel disappointed for the people of Nazareth. There is no record in the Gospels of Jesus ever returning to Nazareth. What a loss for those people! Because of their unbelief, only a few heard the Good News and experienced the healing, freeing, restoring of sight, lifting of burdens, and blessings that Jesus came to bring.

Just as people had a choice 2,000 years ago, they have a choice today. We, as Christian writers, also have a choice. We can accept or reject Jesus' words. We can proclaim the message of freedom that cost Jesus his life, or we can water down the power of the Gospel and the Resurrection.

"Water down the Gospel?" That would never be our intent! Yet, the fact is, that unless we are experiencing firsthand the implications of Jesus' Independence Day proclamation, we will not be as effective as we could be in sharing it with our readers.

We need to ask ourselves if we really understand what Jesus meant by preaching "Good News to the poor." Do we understand the significance of the word *poor*? Do we recognize that without him we are nothing? Do we daily admit our need for him and humbly put our complete trust in him? And do we take time to sit at his feet and learn more about the Good News he wants to impart? "God was in Christ, restoring the world to himself, no longer counting men's sins against them but blotting them out. This is the wonderful message he has given us to tell others" (2 Cor. 5:19, TLB).

Jesus said he came to "heal the brokenhearted." If we are struggling with deep unresolved hurts, or if an unforgiving spirit has enabled resentment and bitterness to get a foothold in our life, then we need to allow God to heal our hearts. He never intended for us to go through life depressed or sapped of our strength by experiences--perhaps some as far back as our childhood--that we could not control and certainly cannot change. He wants to make us whole!

Jesus also said he came to "announce that captives shall be released." *Webster's New Dictionary* defines *captive* as "a person caught and held prisoner." Sometimes, if we are honest with ourselves, we have to admit that we're prisoners to negative thinking patterns, to doubts, to fears, and to feelings of discouragement. Or, we may be prisoners to bad habits. Are we asking him to set us free?

With his touch, Jesus healed many who were blind. I suspect, however, that some of them knew more than just the joy of seeing the earth and sky, trees and people. Undoubtedly, many had their eyes opened to spiritual truths they had never seen before. What about us? Are we seeing things clearly, or is our vision blurred? Do we need him to touch us and heal us so we can see life from his perspective?

The first century Israelites were a people downtrodden by their oppressors. The Romans imposed heavy taxes and quickly quenched any flames--or even sparks--of political unrest or revolution. Today, people are still oppressed by cruel governments and merciless economic systems. On a more personal level, many of us know the oppression that comes from being weighed down by heavy emotional or financial burdens, or from being persecuted for the stand we take as Christians. Others may experience in very real ways the oppression of the evil one. Are we trusting Jesus will give us victory?

Finally, Jesus proclaimed that God was "'ready to give blessings to all who come to him'" (Luke 4:19, TLB). Again, we have to ask ourselves whether we wait long enough in his presence to receive all he has for us. Do we give him "prime time" each day, or do we squeeze him in only when it is convenient or when our needs are desperate?

Jesus' first Independence Day proclamation is filled with promises for us today. As we learn to claim and act on them, we will find our lives filled with new power. Then when we take up our pens to write, God's truth--the truth that truly does set men free--will resound throughout the land.

Responding to God's Call to Write

Prayerfully reflect on Luke 4:18-19 and ask the Lord to show you ways you can more fully experience and write about:

Good News for the poor

Healing for the brokenhearted

Freedom for the captives

Recovering of sight for the blind

Victory for the downtrodden

God's blessings

When I am weak, then I am strong--the less I have,
the more I depend on him.
2 Corinthians 12:10, TLB

19
Confidence

Suddenly everything seemed to be getting in the way of my writing. Other things, good things, were demanding time and energy. I didn't see how I could say "no." When I walked past my office and felt a twinge of guilt, I told myself my hectic schedule was only temporary. Besides, I couldn't let people down when they were depending on me.

One day my writing mentor helped me to see what was happening. "You're running from the very thing you most want to do," she said. "You're running from your writing. Don't you see?" she explained, when I looked puzzled. "New writing opportunities are stretching before you and, to put it bluntly, you're scared. You're protecting yourself from the possibility of failure by becoming so involved with other things that you have an excuse not to write."

She's right. I am afraid of failure, I admitted to myself. *I don't have confidence in my writing ability. And I have been saying "yes" to other things to avoid having to prove myself as a writer.*

"It's a cop-out to see yourself as a failure," she continued, as if reading my thoughts. "You've served your apprenticeship. It's time to move on --to make a commitment to being successful even though success is a lonely and risky thing."

Everyone who is serious about writing will face similar turning points when the choice must be made: Move ahead or turn back. Repeatedly, we will be forced to ask ourselves whether or not we are willing to risk failure.

It is not just beginning writers who feel anxious when starting a new project, or mailing a completed manuscript. Even established writers know their work may not be accepted. Success brings with it a heavier responsibility to produce quality work. Self-expectations, as well as the expectations of editors, become greater. At any moment a "crisis of confidence," as my mentor calls it, can occur.

It can be triggered by many things. We may feel trapped in an interminably long period of writers' block. An editor may require a rewrite of something we felt was our very best work. A manuscript may be returned that we were sure would be accepted. It may even be a manuscript we wrote on assignment. I remember when that happened to me. I was devastated! Besides the blow to my ego, I felt I had let the editor down. He expected me to produce something he could use. I had reached one of those turning points. I could choose to play it safe and turn down future assignments. I could accept them (and even seek them) despite my feelings of inadequacy. Or, I could give up and quit.

I remember flipping through the pages of my Bible. Colossians 1:29 (TLB) leaped out at me: "This is my work, and I can do it only because Christ's mighty energy is at work within me."

Knowing that Paul wrote those words from prison made them even more meaningful to me. I imagined how the evil one must have used that time to try to persuade Paul to question his call. He must have delighted in reminding Paul of past failures, as well as the times of hardship and hostility. Paul's spirit had absorbed rebuffs and criticism, even from fellow Christians. His body carried the scars of beatings and lashings. "Is it worth it?" Satan must have whispered more than once. "If God really called you to be a missionary, then why is he allowing you to rot here in prison?" But Paul chose to remain true to his call to spread the Good News by writing letters that might otherwise not have been written.

But Paul met the Lord on the Damascus Road, I thought to myself. *He knew Jesus more intimately than I do.*

Yes, I could argue that Paul had a greater measure of faith because of these experiences. Yet, he also knew what it meant to go from tremendous spiritual highs to deep lows and to be plagued with a "thorn" in his flesh. If, as some commentators suggest, it was epilepsy or an eye disease, it must have caused Paul to wrestle with doubts. How could he preach if he might have a seizure, or write if he could not see?

God did not remove the thorn. Instead, he told Paul, "'I am with you; that is all you need. My power shows up best in weak people'" (2 Cor. 12:9, TLB). Paul chose to rely on this promise. As a result, he could say, "when I am weak, then I am strong--the less I have, the more I depend on him" (2 Cor. 12:10, TLB).

The cure for a crisis of confidence is to re-examine in what, or more importantly, in whom, we have built our confidence. "I know the one in whom I trust," Paul wrote to Timothy (2 Tim. 1:12, TLB). That's the key. It's not self-confidence, but God-confidence!

"Stir into flame the strength and boldness that is in you," Paul counseled Timothy (2 Tim. 1:6, TLB). Does that mean he expected Timothy should never be afraid? No! "I came to you in weakness--timid and trembling," Paul admitted to the Christians in Corinth (1 Cor. 2:3, TLB). And he didn't go to Corinth until his second missionary journey!

"Stand steady, and don't be afraid of suffering for the Lord," Paul encouraged Timothy. "Bring others to Christ. Leave nothing undone that you ought to do" (2 Tim. 4:5, TLB). The NIV reads, "discharge all the duties of your ministry."

If a crisis of confidence is holding you back from the work you know you have been called to do, it's time to acknowledge that it's not self-confidence you need, but God-confidence. It's time to learn what it means "to be a living demonstration of Christ's power, instead of showing off [your] own power and abilities" (2 Cor. 12:9, TLB).

Responding to God's Call to Write

The child within us urges us not to risk failure. But the Lord encourages us to "put away the childish things" and to respond to his call in "faith, hope, and love" (1 Cor. 13:11,13, TLB).

Faith reminds us that "no one who believes in Christ will ever be disappointed" (Rom. 10:11, TLB). *Hope* affirms that God can work something good from everything--even from failures should our fears be realized (see Rom. 8:28). And *love* compels us to follow Jesus' example--to put aside our own pleasures, shoulder our crosses, and follow him closely (see Mark 8:34).

Do a topical study of the words *faith, hope,* and *love.* Record below verses you find that will help you to persevere during times of doubt and fear.

I want to suggest that you finish what you started to do....
2 Corinthians 8:10, TLB

20
Finish What You Start!

I knew God had called me to write a book. I worked for weeks gathering notes. Using *Books in Print* and catalogs from Christian publishing houses, I did my market research. Almost nothing was available on my topic. I sensed I was ahead of the market, but since the secular press was addressing the issue, I hoped Christian publishers would not be too much farther behind.

The more I worked, the more enthusiastic I became. I saw how my book would meet a real need. I felt the Lord's guidance as the chapter-by-chapter synopsis fell into place. I committed myself, and my book, to the Lord and asked him to help me write it to his glory.

I'd like to say that from that point on everything went smoothly--that I faithfully sat down to write each day, completed my book in record time, found a publisher immediately, and saw it make the best seller list. The truth is I got bogged down and discouraged. My enthusiasm and commitment waned. It became easier and easier to procrastinate.

One morning a passage of Scripture jumped out at me: "I want to suggest that you finish what you started to do....Let your enthusiastic idea at the start be equalled by your realistic action now" (2 Cor. 8:10-11, TLB). I got back to work immediately, but before long discouragement again took over. I didn't doubt God wanted the book written; I doubted my ability to write it. I felt overwhelmed and inadequate and afraid to take the risk of pouring myself into a book--especially a book that meant dealing with painful memories. "And what makes you think you can find a publisher *if* you get it finished?" the evil one taunted me.

A workshop taught by Lee Roddy at a 1980 Christian writers' conference was the turning point. Lee said to the class, "God chose you. As you abide in him, your life with bring forth fruit." On the closing day he prayed that "heaven would be different" because of what we would write. He challenged us, if we felt moved by God, to make a commitment to complete our book within a year. I knew God was speaking to me. With a pounding heart and shaking hand I put my commitment in writing.

During the next year I wished I could squirm out of my commitment. I looked for every possible excuse to keep from working on the book. I wrote short pieces. They were easier and I'd always been able to sell them. Now they started coming back. Lee refused to feel sorry for me. "You must ask and seek God's reason. I can offer a suggestion: It's time for you to move on."

Finally, with only three months left, I knew I needed to get busy or I wouldn't make it. Some days I felt all I had to give God was my willingness to be used. But it was enough! With his help, I completed the book--exactly to the day! I mailed it to a publisher I had previously queried. For five months I counted the days and prayed. The more time passed, the more I felt certain they were going to accept it. But one day, the mailman knocked on the door and handed me a package. My heart sank. It was my manuscript with a "Sorry this doesn't meet our needs" note.

The process began all over again. Over a six year period, I queried forty-one publishers! Many of them requested the manuscript only to return it. But God kept encouraging me to send it out again, and he kept giving me promises to sustain me. I remember one especially: "And let us not get tired of doing what is right, for after a while we will reap a harvest of blessing if we don't get discouraged and give up" (Gal. 6:9, TLB). I circled and dated it. The next day the book came back. It had reached the final stages of the review process where one in three manuscripts are accepted. I don't think I would have been able to start all over again with the query process (and do yet another rewrite) if it had not been for that promise and others.

I vividly remember the night a well-meaning friend said, "It seems to me that if God wanted your book published, it would be in print by now." Somehow I managed to bite my tongue and not let her know how angry her words made me. How dare we assume that if God is in something, he will "bless it" by making everything quick and easy when he did not spare even his own Son from taking the difficult and painful road to the cross?

Another friend suggested I had written the book for "practice." I felt like throwing the manuscript at her. I gritted my teeth and plodded on.

More out of habit than hope, I talked to editors at writers' conferences. I about had my "sales pitch" memorized. Most always they asked me to send the manuscript. My postage bill was getting astronomical--and so was my discouragement as the manuscript kept coming back.

Finally my "Please, Lord, let the book be accepted" prayers began to change. "It's your manuscript, Lord. Let your will, not mine, be done." Each time I prayed that prayer the pain of rejection diminished and the conviction grew that God was still in control.

I heard about a new publishing house. I planned to query them. Then, to my surprise, the editor attended my home conference. I made an appointment to talk to him. He took the manuscript with him. When he called several months later and asked me to meet with him to talk about the manuscript, I was stunned. When he added, "And we'll sign the contract at the same time," I was speechless.

When I received the page proofs, terror gripped me. Did I really want to make myself that vulnerable? I considered calling my editor and saying, "Let's forget this." Yet, if even one person could be helped...

My first television interview was equally terrifying. "Why did you write this book?" Jim McClellan asked me. My mind went blank! Praise God, what seemed like an eternity must have been only seconds, and I must have answered intelligently because he asked me to come back.

Now I know why it took six years and three months to find a publisher. I thought back then I was ready for the media interviews and speaking that go with writing a book on a sensitive issue. Now I'm not at all sure I'm ready. But that's growth!

"There is a right time for everything" (Eccl. 3:1, TLB). "We will reap a harvest of blessing if we don't get discouraged and give up" (Gal. 6:9, TLB).

Responding to God's Call to Write

Is there something you've started that you need to finish? To keep you keeping on, read the following passages about the struggles the apostle Paul endured. Record what you feel God is saying to you.

Galatians 1:13--2:1

2 Corinthians 4:8-18

2 Corinthians 6:3-10

2 Corinthians 11:23-33

And the Lord said to me,
"Write my answer on a billboard, large and clear,
so that anyone can read it at a glance
and rush to tell the others.
But these things I plan won't happen right away.
Slowly, steadily, surely, the time approaches
when the vision will be fulfilled.
If it seems slow, do not despair,
for these things will surely come to pass.
Just be patient!
They will not be overdue a single day!"
Habakkuk 2:2-3, TLB

Bible Study Helps
Called to Write His Answer

AND THE LORD SAID TO ME
Press on to know the Lord (Hos. 6:3).
Make time to allow the Lord to speak to you through his Word (Ps. 1:2; 2 Tim. 3:16-17; James 1:25).
Seek his counsel and wisdom (Ps. 16:7; 32:8; Prov. 2:3-10; Isa. 50:4; James 1:5-8).
Wait for God's answer (Hab. 2:1).
Let his words sink into your heart first (Ezek. 3:10-11) and then write what you have experienced (1 John 1:3).

WRITE MY ANSWER
Diligently study the Word (2 Tim. 2:15).
Remember the promise--his Word does not return void (Isa. 55:11).
Put on the armor (Eph. 6:10-18).
Make the most of your opportunities (Eph. 5:15-17; Phil. 2:15-16; Col. 4:5-6; 2 Tim. 4:2) knowing that the doors may not always be open (Amos 8:11-12).

MAKE IT LARGE AND CLEAR
Write to be understood and to make the Gospel clear (1 Cor. 2:1-5).
Let the Holy Spirit do the convicting--don't preach (1 Cor. 2:4; Heb. 4:12).
Know your audience. Communicate on their level (1 Cor. 2:6).
Work hard (Col. 3:23-24), and enthusiastically (Rom. 12:11), so you do not need to be ashamed of your work (2 Tim. 2:15) or to compare it with others (Gal. 6:4).

WRITE SO THAT ANYONE CAN READ IT
Share the Good News around the world (Ps. 96:1-3; Matt. 28:19-20).
Following Christ's example, minister to the poor, brokenhearted, captives, blind, downtrodden (Luke 4:18-19).
Use illustrations readers can relate to (Mark 4:33-34).

AT A GLANCE
Have a clear focus--know what you believe and clearly communicate it (1 Cor. 1:30; 2 Tim. 1:11-12).
Capture the reader's attention and create reader identification (Mark 4:2).

AND RUSH TO TELL OTHERS
Write so that readers will want to pass it on. Be winsome (1 Thess. 2:7-8; James 3:17).
Provide a take away so readers will not ask, "So what?" (James 1:22).
Avoid Christian cliches, pat answers, theological jargon (1 Cor. 1:17).

SLOWLY, STEADILY, SURELY
Seek God's plan for your writing (Jer. 29:11-13).
Set specific and measurable goals (Prov. 16:9).
Get to work (1 Chron. 28:20).
Abide in him (John 15:4-8).
Keep expecting him to help you; walk (and write) in his strength (Ps. 71:14,16).
Give yourself and your writing time to develop (Rom. 5:2; Phil. 1:6; Co 2:7; 2 Pet. 1:2-8).
Have faith (Matt. 21:21-22; John 14:12-14; Heb. 11:1).
Finish what you start (2 Cor. 8:10-11).
Do NOT give in to discouragement and despair (Gal. 6:9).

Laying a Biblical Foundation
for Your Writing Ministry

I will press on to know the Lord (Hos. 6:3), abide in him (John 15:1-8), and keep on growing in him (Col. 2:6-7; 2 Pet. 1:2-9).

I will keep my eyes on Jesus, my leader and instructor (Heb. 12:2).

I will diligently study God's Word in order to become an effective communicator of his truth (2 Tim. 2:15; 3:16-17).

I will daily seek the infilling of the Holy Spirit (Acts 1:8; Eph. 5:18).

I will spend time in prayer--especially in learning to be still and to listen to what God may want to say to me and through me (Ps. 5:3; 46:10; Hab. 2:1; 1 Cor. 2:16).

I will make a commitment to private and corporate worship (Ps. 99:5; Heb. 10:25).

I will seek God's direction for my life and for my writing (Ps. 32:8; Jer. 29:11-13; Gal. 5:16; James 1:5-8).

I will be sensitive to needs around me and say "yes" to God's call to write his answer (Hab. 2:2).

I will wait on God's empowering (Ps. 40:1-3; Isa. 40:29-31; Col. 1:29).

I will use the gift God has given me and work hard (1 Tim. 4:14-15; 2 Tim. 2:15; 1 Pet. 4:10-11).

I will set specific, measurable goals (Prov. 16:9).

I will reach out to other Christian writers both to give and to receive support and encouragement (Gal. 6:2; 1 Thess. 5:11).

I will humble myself before the Lord and ask forgiveness for my sins that I might be a cleansed vessel through which his power can flow (Prov. 28:13; James 4:7-10; 1 Pet. 5:6; 1 John 1:8-10).

I will put on the armor (Eph. 6:10-17) and stand firm when the evil one attacks (1 Pet. 5:8-9).

I will ask for wisdom in setting daily priorities and in keeping my life in balance (Prov. 2:3-10).

I will battle procrastination (Eccl. 5:7), get to work (1 Chron. 28:20), and finish what I start (2 Cor. 8:10-11).

I will stay awake and be prepared for his return (Matt. 25:13) and make the most of every opportunity (Col. 4:5).

I will see the rough times in my life as an opportunity to grow (Rom. 5:3-5; James 1:2-4) and to pass on to others God's help and comfort (2 Cor. 1:3-7).

I will seek first his Kingdom and his righteousness (Matt. 6:33; Luke 12:31) and trust him to supply all my needs (Phil. 4:19).

I will not get discouraged and give up (Gal. 6:9) but instead will persist and trust God's perfect timing (Ps. 27:14; 37:7; 42:11; Eccl. 3:1; Hab. 2:3; Heb. 11:1)

I will affirm that now I have "every grace and blessing; every spiritual gift and power for doing his will" (1 Cor. 1:7, TLB) and expect God to do great things through his power at work within me (Eph. 3:20).

From Idea to Published Manuscript

1.   Train yourself to find ideas in the Scriptures, life experiences, history, nature, the media, etc.

2.   Capture your idea immediately by writing it down. Keep a journal.

3.   File your ideas in notebooks, card files, manila folders, or envelopes. Develop a corresponding resource file.

4.   Ask yourself which ideas you feel most compelled to develop.

5.   Pray about your ideas.   Ask the Lord to help you weed out the "fluff" and to show you which of the others should take priority. Work them into your Goal Planning Chart (see page 24) and writing schedule.

6.   Research the market (see Writers' Helps, page 95).

7.   Before you begin writing, picture your reader and pray for him. Consider Lee Roddy's acrostic, *BERT,* for an effective manuscript. How will it *Benefit* and *Enrich* your reader? Is it *Relevant* and *Timely?*

8.   Determine the best format for your idea--story, article, devotional, poem, or perhaps even a book. Be realistic. Know the best opportunities.

9.   Do the necessary research--the Scriptures, quotes from books or articles, interviews. Quote accurately and get permission when needed.

10. Outline or develop a plan for your manuscript.

11. Write and rewrite as many times as necessary until you are certain this is your very best work. (This is where it helps to have input from other writers. *Christian Writers' Market Guide* has a list of workshops.)

12. Ask yourself: Do I have a clear theme or story line? Is my idea tightly focused and well organized? Is there reader identification and a strong take-away? Have I been open, honest, vulnerable? Did I show or tell? Teach or preach?

13. Resist the temptation to mail it too soon. Let it "cool" for a week. Live it!

14. Put your best foot forward. Show you have carefully studied the market by submitting a manuscript that will meet their editorial needs. Be sure to use the proper manuscript format and enclose a SASE.

15. Do the needed recordkeeping to keep track of submissions.

16. As you mail your manuscript, release it to the Lord and get to work on your next writing project. Be sure to get a receipt from the post office and note this in your log of writing expenses/earnings.

17. If your manuscript is returned, resubmit it immediately to the next name on your list. Do not give in to the temptation to doubt your work. Do not rewrite until it's been out at least three times.

18. After publication pray for the editor and his ministry, and for the people who will read your printed piece. Learn all you can from the changes the editor made. Send a brief thank you letter and another manuscript or query. Be a good steward by marketing reprints of your first rights work.

19. Do not give in to the deadly D's--disappointment, discouragement, doubt, and despair. Look to Jesus. Remember he never promised it would be easy to follow him. Claim the promise of Galatians 6:9 and persevere.

20. Keep developing your skills. Keep growing. Attend writing seminars and conferences (see list in *Christian Writers' Market Guide*). Consider enrolling in a correspondence school (see Writers' Helps, page 95).

Writers' Helps

MAGAZINES AND NEWSLETTERS

The Christian Communicator. PO Box 827, San Juan Capistrano, CA
  92675. Monthly.
Cross & Quill. 590 W. Mercers Fernery Road, DeLand, FL 32770.
  Bi-monthly publication of Christian Writers Fellowship International.
Channels and *Currents.* Three times a year. Christian Writers League
  of America, Rt. 2, Box 366A, Harlingen, TX 78550.
Living Streams. Quarterly. PO Box 1321, Vincennes, IN 47591.
Writers Information Network. Elaine Colvin, Director, PO Box 11337,
  Bainbridge Island, WA 98110. Bi-monthly.

BOOKS

Anderson, Margaret. *The Christian Writers Handbook.* Harper & Row.
Butler, Marie. *The Wedging.* Troika Ministries, 6927 NW 78th St.,
  Kansas City, MO 64152.
Duncan, Lois. *How to Write and Sell Your Personal Experiences.* Writer's
  Digest.
Franzen, Janice Gosnell. *The Adventure of Interviewing.* Christian
  Writers Institute.
Gentz, William. *Religious Writers Marketplace.* Running Press.
  Writing to Inspire. Writer's Digest.
Guidebook to Successful Christian Writing. Christian Writers Institute.
Hensley, Dennis and Adkins, Rose. *Writing for Religious and Other
  Specialty Markets.* Broadman Press.
Hensley, Dennis and Miller, Holly. *The Freelance Writers Handbook.*
  Harper & Row.
Herr, Ethel. *An Introduction to Christian Writing.* Tyndale House.

Holmes, Marjorie. *Writing the Creative Article.* The Writer.
Hudson, Bob and Townsend, Shelley. *A Christian Writer's Manual of Style.* Zondervan.
Klug, Ronald. *How to Keep a Spiritual Journal.* Thomas Nelson.
Miller, Holly. *How to Earn More than Pennies for Your Thoughts.* Warner Press.
Provost, Gary. *Beyond Style.* Writer's Digest.
Make Every Word Count. Writer's Digest.
Ricks, Chip and Marsh, Marilyn. *How to Write for Christian Magazines.* Broadman Press.
Shedd, Charlie. *If I Can Write, You Can Write.* Writer's Digest.
Stuart, Sally. *Christian Writers' Market Guide.* Joy Publishing.
A Marketing Plan for More Sales. Joy Publishing.
Strunk, William Jr. *The Elements of Style.* MacMillan.
Thoene, Bodie and Brock. *Writer to Writer.* Bethany House.
Vaughn, Ruth. *Write to Discover Yourself.* Doubleday-Galilee.
Walker, Robert. *Leads and Story Openings.* Creation House.
Watkins, James. *The Persuasive Person.* Wesley Press.
Wirt, Sherwood. *Getting Into Print.* Thomas Nelson.
The Making of a Writer. Augsburg.
You Can Tell the World. Augsburg.
Wyndham, Lee. *Writing for Children and Teenagers.* Writer's Digest.
Young, Woody. *Copyright Law--What You Don't Know Can Co$t You.* Joy Publishing.
Zinsser, William. *On Writing Well.* Harper & Row.

CHRISTIAN WRITING CORRESPONDENCE SCHOOLS
Christian Writers Guild. Norman Rohrer, director. 260 Fern Lane, Hume, CA 93628-9889.
Christian Writers Institute. Robert Walker, founder and president. 388 E. Gundersen Drive, Wheaton, IL 60188.
Christian Writers Fellowship International. Mary Harwell Sayler, director. 590 W. Mercers Fernery Road, Deland, FL 32780.

ALSO BY THE AUTHOR
Ministry/Marketing Packet. Bible studies, time management helps, how-to's for effective marketing, writers' check-off lists, and more.
ABC's of Marketing. How-to's of market research and analysis, best opportunities, five market analysis charts, and more.
Tapes on a variety of writing related topics with study sheets.
For more information and prices write:
Marlene Bagnull, 316 Blanchard Road, Drexel Hill, PA 19026.